The Creative Classroom

A
Guide
for Using
Creative Drama
in the
Classroom,
PreK-6

WRITTEN & COMPILED BY
Lenore Blank Kelner

HEINEMANN
Portsmouth, NH

Heinemann

361 Hanover Street
Portsmouth, NH 03801-3912
Offices and agents throughout the world

Editor: Lisa A. Barnett
Production: Renee Le Verrier and Nancy Sheridan
Text and cover design: Joni Doherty

Many of the activities in this book were first published in a curriculum document entitled *A Practical Guide for Using Creative Drama in the Classroom*, by Lenore Blank. Published 1985 by the Baltimore County Public Schools, Towson, Maryland.

Acknowledgments and credit lines begin on page ix.

Library of Congress Cataloging-in-Publication Data
Kelner, Lenore Blank.
    The creative classroom : a guide for using creative drama in the classroom, PreK–6 / written and compiled by Lenore Blank Kelner.
        p.   cm.
    Includes bibliographical references.
    ISBN 0-435-08628-6
    1. Drama in education   I. Title
PN3171.K355   1993
372. 13'32—dc20   93-29149
                                                                CIP

Printed on acid-free paper in the United States of America.
Sheridan 2018

This book is dedicated to the memory of
Alvan August Testoni
(1926–1988)

Contents

7

Literature Enrichment & Extension Activities: Story Dramatization 123

8

Strategies for Developing Creative Thinking: Playbuilding (Storybuilding) 171

Acknowledgments

The author and publisher wish to thank the following for permission to reprint copyrighted and previously published material in this book:

"Imaginary Door," "Imaginary Mask," "Coffee Can Theatre" ("Story Can Theatre"), "Playbuilding," and "Role Play" were originally printed in Wolf Trap Institute for Early Learning Through the Arts' (Vienna, VA) publication *Wake Your Wishes Up*, a creative drama handbook for preschool teachers.

"Imaginary Door" was adapted from "Imaginary Gift," created by creative drama specialist Michelle Valeri, Silver Spring, MD.

"Imaginary Mask" was adapted from "Bag Full of Masks," created by storyteller Marc Spiegel, Washington, DC.

"Story Can Theatre" was adapted from "Coffee Can Theatre," created by actor Michael Littman, Lincoln, NH.

"Side by Side" was adapted from "Back to Back," created by educator Judy D'Onfrio, Baltimore, MD.

"The Magical Tree" is adapted from "The Tale of the Name of the Tree" in *Bantu Tales* by Pattie Price, ©1938 by E.P. Dutton. Reprinted in adapted form as "The Tale of the Name Tree" in *Around the World Story Book* by Danny Kaye. Copyright ©1960. Published by Random House.

"Bits 'n' Pieces," "Change Three," "Pass the Eraser," and "Transforming the Object" were adapted from "Parts of a Whole," "Three Changes," "Name Six," and "Object Transformation," from *Improvisation for the Theater* by Viola Spolin. Copyright ©1963. Published by Northwestern University Press.

"The ABC Game," "Becoming Objects," "Environment Orchestra," "Grandmother's Trunk," "Name It!," "Plants on the Grow," "Sound Trip," "Spell It!," "Then What Happened?," "Texture Walk/Mobile Words," and "Magic Box" were adapted from "Alphabet Adjectives," "The Apartment," "Sounds Like," "Grandmother's Trunk," "Name It!" "Pumpkin Patch," "Sound Trip," "Spell It!," "Then What Happened?," "Texture Walk/Mobile Words," and "Magic Box" from *Have You Roared Today? A Creative Drama Handbook*. Copyright © 1979 by Montgomery County Public Schools, Title 1, ESEA, Rockville, MD.

A special thanks to Karen Murray, Paula Sutton, Judy D'Onofrio, and the Baltimore County (Maryland) Chapter I resource teachers and staff.

A very special thanks to Paul Kelner for all his help and support through the years.

An Overview

This book consists of 51+ creative drama activities that can be easily incorporated into ongoing classroom instruction. These activities introduce, review, and reinforce content material across the curriculum. They are designed to complement, supplement, and augment your existing lesson plans.

No prior theatre or creative drama training or experience is needed to use these activities effectively. They are uncomplicated, and this booklet provides you with step-by-step procedural outlines and actual scripts to make implementation smooth.

The book is divided into eight chapters: "An Overview"; "Activities for Review and Reinforcement"; "Strategies for Grammar and Spelling"; "Classifying and Sequencing Techniques"; "Activities That Deepen Comprehension and Promote Writing Skills: Visualization"; "Activities That Promote Language and Thinking Skills: Role Play"; "Literature Enrichment and Extension Activities: Story Dramatization"; and "Strategies for Developing Creative Thinking: Playbuilding (Storybuilding)." As you read and become familiar with each chapter you will see how the activities can be used in many different ways. For instance, some of the classifying techniques also build vocabulary, and many of the activities can be used as prewriting techniques or as oral composing activities.

Often trying something new in the classroom feels uncomfortable. "Will I lose control?" "How can I maintain my position of authority?" "Will the children take advantage of me?" These comments are often made by teachers when first introduced to creative drama. These are important concerns. This book will address these concerns in the section "Guidelines for Success" by providing detailed suggestions and strategies for maintaining control.

Once you have made the commitment to try your first activity, it is extremely important that you structure it carefully. Your first attempt should be as comfortable for you as possible. For example, the first activity you try may last only five minutes. The next one may last longer or may not. You may choose at first to schedule the activities before lunch, recess, or dismissal if you are concerned the class might get over stimulated. The important point is to try the activities in a way that suits you.

Your students will grow and risk in increments as well. They need time in order to comprehend fully what is being asked of them. Once students are clear and comfortable, their creativity will blossom.

As students get older, the imagination often is associated with "kids' stuff." It becomes more difficult for them to imagine. But the child still lives in all of us, and with time it will emerge. Don't be discouraged if, initially, the results are not particularly exciting—they will be. Begin with the simple activities and progress to those that involve more risk taking. Eventually the responses from your students will be impressive.

Why is all this important? Because these activities *really* work. They motivate students to learn by grabbing their attention and by physically involving them in learning. They are entertaining but extremely educational. They are refreshing for teachers because they provide new ways to approach old and sometimes stale subject matter. Teachers who have used these activities are thrilled by their success.

You are encouraged to develop, modify, and improve upon these activities to make them a true extension of your teaching style. As every teacher has a unique and valid style, it is vital that these activities truly become your own.

What Is Creative Drama?

Before putting these activities into action, it's important to have a clear definition of creative drama. Creative drama essentially is a form of imaginative play. That is why students and teachers respond to it with so much enthusiasm. All people love to have fun and to use their imaginations.

Creative drama differs from random play because it is facilitated by a leader or teacher who attempts to structure the play into a definite form. Often this form consists of a beginning, a middle, and a conclusion. By emphasizing form, the teacher takes amorphous and random play and elevates it to the educational domain.

Creative drama is improvisational. It is created on the spot. It is not scripted. The result is the spontaneous self-expression of the individual. This is a key goal of creative dramatics. The students may reenact a story that they have read; but through creative drama, it is performed in their own words to convey their own meanings. It is not memorized. This process allows students to synthesize and to translate various educational concepts into a personally meaningful form.

The results are often astounding. Students who seem distracted or disinterested come to life when their imaginations are tapped. Teachers are often amazed at the vocabulary and knowledge these students have internalized but may not have previously shared. Oral composing skills are strong in creative drama. Whole language experts acknowledge that oral composing is the rehearsal for written composition. Therefore, creative drama can give teachers a fresh perspective of their students' abilities while also preparing students for writing.

Since the process is spontaneous and not rehearsed, it is often crudely performed. There are few, if any, props or costumes. A suggestive prop or costume may be helpful but is rarely essential. A polished performance is *not* the goal of creative dramatics. It is not meant to be seen by an audience. The process is solely for the experience of the participants. Neither the teacher nor the students need to be theatre experts, because the success of the activity is not measured by the level of theatrical skill but instead by the creative expression it promotes.

Note the word "process" has been used often in this definition. Creative drama is process-centered rather than product-centered. The success of an activity is not measured by the beauty of the outcome as in a theatrical production, but by the ideas, risks, and inventiveness it elicits.

Focusing on a process of learning may be quite different from some present-day educational practice. Educators often stress only the products of education: How fast do the students read? Did they pass the test? Do they know their multiplication tables? Can they spell? Of course, this product-minded philosophy has its place and importance. However, every teacher

An Overview

knows that all students do not learn in the same way. Students have a variety of learning styles, and therefore students respond differently to various teaching methods. Often it is precisely "the how," the process by which a teacher presents information, that makes all the difference in the world as to whether or not a student is successful.

All of the creative drama strategies found in this book use multisensory involvement. The students are chanting, moving, listening, and speaking as they learn. Due to the multisensory component of these games, students with all learning styles respond to these activities and can, therefore, succeed in learning.

Clearly school systems must not underestimate the effect of coupling a creative process with traditional teaching strategies. By using creative drama, educators can discover new and stimulating tools for teaching—tools that convey the facts as well as allow students and teachers to explore their own creativity.

What Are the Benefits of Using Creative Drama in the Classroom?

In addition to motivating students and providing alternative classroom techniques for teachers, creative drama has other educational benefits. Listed below are some of the ways creative drama can help teachers accomplish many of their educational objectives.

CREATIVE DRAMA

▶ *Stimulates the imagination and promotes creative thinking.*
Many students today have limited imaginations. They cannot envision images other than those fed to them by television or movies. New vistas can be visualized through creative drama.

▶ *Develops critical thinking skills.*
Activities are often open-ended. They provide students with opportunities for predicting and problem solving.

▶ *Promotes language development.*
All of the techniques are designed to develop expressive and receptive language skills. They motivate students to speak and therefore are perfect for ESL students and students with language delay. The retelling and reenacting of stories are excellent oral composing activities that prepare students for the writing process.

- *Heightens effective listening skills.*

  When viewing television, students are stimulated on an average of every three to four seconds by a different visual image on the screen. Images of a TV commercial change on an average of every two to three seconds.[1] Video games and computer graphics stimulate at an even faster rate. Is it any wonder, then, that students have difficulty being attentive to one teacher in front of the classroom for six hours?

  Television is a visual medium; we *watch* television.[2] Often the words are insignificant, or we tune them out. Since students spend so much time *watching* television, their auditory skills are often poor. Anything that is not visually entertaining, *i.e.*, the classroom, is often blocked out. Therefore our students have trouble listening, following directions, creating mental images, associating ideas, and conceptualizing. Television does not promote the development of these skills. Creative drama activities can help students progress in these important learning areas.

- *Strengthens comprehension and learning retention by involving the senses as an integral part of the learning process.*
  Research has shown that sensory involvement consistently increases learning comprehension. Creative drama is multi-sensory and highly experiential. By using these strategies in the classroom, teachers help to meet the needs of students with varying learning styles.

- *Increases empathy and awareness of others.*
  Creative drama provides a vehicle for exploring values and feelings by reenacting various characters and their behaviors. It also allows students to explore and experience the consequences of behavior.

- *Fosters peer respect and group cooperation.*
  Each student contributes something unique to an activity, which leads to a strong sense of group appreciation. Cliques and tensions that may exist within a class can be diminished and often eliminated through these games.

---

[1] Neil Postman, *The Disappearance of Childhood.* New York: Laurel Press, 1982, p.78.

[2] *Ibid.*

- *Reinforces positive self-concept.*

  A fundamental concept of creative drama is self-expression. Individual perceptions and interpretations are sought, supported, and sincerely valued. The experience leads students to receive positive reinforcement for their unique contributions, enabling them to feel successful. Success breeds success, just as failure breeds failure. Providing students with a forum for success can help them build confidence that may transfer to other areas of learning.

- *Provides teachers with a fresh perspective on teaching.*

  By coupling creative drama activities with existing lessons, teachers discover new ways to approach old material. This can be stimulating, challenging, and uplifting. It can prevent the feeling of burnout.

For all of these reasons, creative drama can be a valuable addition to classroom instruction. ". . . (It) aids, rather than interferes, with other study and achievement."[3]

Guidelines for Success

Now that creative drama has been defined and its benefits clarified, let's focus on its practical applications. As mentioned in the introduction, this section will provide you with a number of guidelines and specific strategies for successful implementation of the activities. Success, in relation to creative drama, is measured by maintaining a balance between discipline (control) and the fostering of creativity. The following guidelines should help you to find that balance.

Creative Environment *versus* Discipline

Setting the appropriate tone for these activities is important. If students are to trust that they can freely express themselves in an exercise, you must set the proper mood. Patience is important. Talking slowly and quietly helps to calm students. It must be a nurturing environment—one that is free of sarcasm.

An important factor in setting the proper tone is that you take the first risk. You need to do the activity first. Once you have demonstrated the activity for your students, the expectations become clear. The students feel safe in trying the activity, too.

---

[3] Brian Way, *Development through Drama*. London: Longman Group Limited, 1967, p. 7.

Encourage all students to participate but *do not force any to do so.* Students, in general, will participate when ready and only at that time. Forcing them can push them away instead of bringing them closer to taking a risk. Their autonomy must be respected, even validated, so that they can develop trust. Sometimes providing introverted students with several optional answers from which to choose can help them take the first step.

Try not to correct any response unless *absolutely necessary.* Try to accept all responses or in some way make the student feel successful. If an error is made concerning factual information in any of the games, try to generalize it as "something the class may need to work on" or "we all can get that confused." Search for a way, including modifying the activity for an individual student, so that all students have some measure of success. Use applause as often as possible. After each student has a turn, you can use applause as a reinforcer. If you use it, be sure *everyone* gets a hand. However, sometimes a student or a group of students may present something extraordinary. If that is the case, feel free to give them a standing ovation.

Although the atmosphere needs to be nurturing, discipline is also essential. Feel free to set ground rules that are comfortable for you. For example, at the outset simply say: "Today we are going to use our imagination and play some exciting games. Those of you who don't follow directions may not be able to participate."

If students need to be removed from the activity, simply and quietly tap them on the shoulder and tell them to take their seats or sit elsewhere, alone in the room, until they are ready to participate. Try to keep the students in the room so that they can watch. As they observe the fun the class is having, they will long to rejoin the group. This is a great behavior modifier. The beauty of creative drama is that it becomes more fun for students to participate than for them to misbehave. The ever-present power struggles between teachers and students tend to diminish during these activities. Often students who have been removed are ready to reenter the activity within a matter of minutes.

Periodically there will be a student who challenges the activity. The student will deny seeing anything imaginary: "I don't see any magic door!" or "There's no imaginary pizza!" or "I don't see (hear) anything!" The best response I have found to counter and halt this negative attitude has been: "You're right, there is nothing there. You'll only see (hear) it if you use your imagination. Otherwise, there is nothing there." This statement usually shocks the student and ends the power struggle he or she may be trying to create.

If the class, as a whole, gets over-stimulated by an activity, simply stop the action, have them close their eyes, and explain quietly that their behavior is not appropriate. Tell them they will get another chance at the activity and to improve their behavior at a later date. Then stop the activity and try it again the next day.

This will usually help the students to respond appropriately to new activities. However, if the class is a very active one, try the activity in small groups first. If the game is done with small groups, be sure to promise the entire class a chance to play the game. If only select students get to participate, there will be resentment.

Eventually the entire class will be able to play the game at one time. Since the activities are so enjoyable, the students will want to cooperate. The activities can also serve as a reward for the class if they all finish their work or pass a test.

Preset the Activity

Before beginning any creative drama activity involving the imagination, the class must be prepared. The students must be informed as to what they are going to do, what is expected of them, and how the activity will work. They need to know before the activity begins that they are expected to pretend to be other people or work with objects that are not really there. In this book, this preparation is referred to as *preset*. (If you are not sure that your students understand the words "pretend" or "imagination," do the "Food Pantomime" activity as a way to give them a hands-on experience with these concepts.)

In the preset section of an activity, you start with reality and prepare the students for the fantasy portion of the lesson. Here is an example of a preset for "Story Can Theatre":

What's this? That's right, it's a coffee can. (Reality) *Well, I used all the coffee that came in this can. And now, if we use our imaginations and pretend, a friend of mine who lives in the can will come out and talk to us.* (Fantasy) *Are you ready to meet her?*

Taking the students clearly from reality to fantasy and then back to reality helps the children know what to expect and also helps calm them down at the end of the activity.

Another good way to prepare students for an imaginative lesson is to have the students close their eyes. Here is an example of a preset using this technique:

Today we are going to use our imaginations. We're going to New York City, and we're going to see all the sights we have studied about in our unit on New York.

Now I'd like you to close your eyes, sit comfortably, and when I count to three, we won't be in our classroom anymore (Reality). *Instead we will be in front of the Statue of Liberty* (Fantasy). *One, two, three . . .*

Having students close their eyes and wait for you to count is a great control device. It tends to focus them on the task and calm them down. It also unifies the class and prepares them for what is to come. It can be used at anytime during the activity to change locations, moods, or simply to quiet the class.

Close the Activity

Often this is forgotten, but it is an essential step in any successful creative drama activity in which students are asked to use their imaginations. If the students have been asked to go to an imaginary place or become other people, they must be returned to reality at the end of the activity. If they are not brought back to the real world, they will be disoriented, distracted, unable to do other classroom work, and will constantly refer to the activity as if it is still going on. Since you started with reality and then moved to fantasy, you must also bring them back home. Here is an example of how to close an activity that can be used over and over again:

You did a great job! Now close your eyes. . . . Close your eyes. . . . When I count to three, we will no longer be at (place) *and/or no longer be* (characters), *instead we will be ourselves again, back in our classroom. One, two, three . . .*

As you develop your own methods of closing the activity, *please* do not say:

"We will be back in our classroom ready to go to work."

This implies that the activity you just completed was not classroom work or that it had little educational value. This tends to reinforce the students' feelings that learning cannot be fun. The purpose of these activities is to prove the opposite.

Needless to say, that even with providing closure, there may be a few stragglers who say, "I'm still the king," or "I'm still on top of the volcano." To these few, simply say:

"I'm sorry you didn't come back with the rest of the class. We've finished using our imaginations. I hope you will join us soon."

Then let the subject drop. This statement doesn't deny the students their illusions, but it does deny them the power struggle they may be trying to set up. They will soon join the real world.

Here is a true story that illustrates perfectly the importance of closure. A group of teachers who had participated in several of my staff development workshops planned a President's Day Assembly at their school for the second grade. When the children came to the program, the teachers preset the children. They asked the children to close their eyes and go back in time to the days of President Lincoln and told them that when they opened their eyes they would meet Abraham Lincoln.

When the children opened their eyes, in front of them stood the vice principal. He was dressed as Abraham Lincoln. He addressed the children as Abe Lincoln, spoke to them about his life and times, and then answered their questions. The children were spellbound. When the time allotted for the assembly was over, the teachers simply dismissed the students! When the students returned to class, some were unable to focus on anything. They were chattery, disoriented, and constantly referring back to the assembly, saying, "Who was that really?" and "Is Mr. X really Abe Lincoln?" and "Is it still 1863?"

Finally, one teacher remembered the concept of closure. She asked her students to close their eyes and brought them back to reality. The students were fine afterward. They settled down and were able to focus on other matters. Those teachers will probably never forget to put closure on a creative drama lesson again.

Imaginary Microphone/Freeze Powder/Imaginary Sleeping Potion

The best control devices are those that are a direct extension of the activity being conducted. If the control device is creative and fun, the students will be more than willing to cooperate. One extremely successful control device has been the imaginary microphone (see "Object Transformation/Playbuilding,

Lesson Two"). Create an imaginary microphone that must be used by the students in order to question a character involved in an activity. You hold the microphone at all times. Stipulating that each student must speak into the microphone in order to be heard eliminates talking out of turn and over-stimulation. The students love it! It reminds them of a television talk show and, therefore, has an adult flair. The microphone can be totally imaginary or made out of a tissue roll, a flashlight, or even an eraser. Do not use a real microphone.

Freeze powder is also great. Simply explain to the students that you possess a special powder that, when sprinkled on them, causes all action to freeze. Practice a few times with the students. Tell them to move, sprinkle the powder, and say, "Freeze!" All action should stop. Say "Melt!" and tell them that word releases the power of the freeze powder. When they hear "Melt!" the action can continue. If, during a scene, the action gets too large and noisy, simply sprinkle on the powder and say, "Freeze!" They'll respond. While the students are "frozen," feel free to redirect the scene to your specifications. Coach them and tell them what needs to happen next or remind them of your ground rules (see "Acting Out a Story").

An imaginary sleeping potion works well when protagonists in an activity get a little carried away. Simply sprinkle them with sleeping dust or give them a sleeping potion, and it will calm them down. They will immediately go to sleep. You'll be surprised.

Many teachers develop their own creative control devices. A third-grade teacher invented a special magic powder that she sprinkled on her students before they wrote. She told the class it would make them more creative. Each time they wrote, she'd go to her desk, get her empty jar and sprinkle the class as they waited patiently. At the end of a writing session she collected the powder and put it back in her jar.

One day, a student refused to return the powder. He said he was going to take it home in order to turn his brother into a frog. Thinking fast, the teacher said, "Oh well, that's okay. The powder loses its effect after 30 minutes." Reluctantly, the student turned in his magic dust.

As you use the activities, you too will become more creative and spontaneous. Devices like these become easy to invent. They work well and are good vehicles for maintaining the balance of creativity and control.

Violence and Television

Inevitably violence will become one of the first topics that will need to be addressed. In any storybuilding activity, the first thing the students will want to do to any adversary is: "Kill him!" "Cut his head, throat, arms, legs," and so on. They see violence on television. In fact, that is basically all they see. Every television program has the same basic formula: "Hit before you get hit, hurt before you get hurt, and kill before you get killed." In other words, "Get the other guy before he gets you!"

Some drama specialists ignore the topic of violence. I try to address the topic head-on. When I am storybuilding with students, I do not accept violence as a means of solving a problem.

Feel free to state, as one of the ground rules, that: "Violence cannot be used in this story." In addition, you could add the following ground rule: "No character in this story (activity) can come from a television program."

This may stun the students at first. They may think there is no way to solve a problem other than by using violence, super-heroes, or television characters. Give them time. They'll come up with an alternative. By setting these ground rules, the students are forced to do some independent thinking and creative problem solving. They cannot rely on familiar answers or pat formulas. These rules elevate the activity to a higher-level learning and thinking experience. This is where creativity begins.

Checklist for Success

In order to implement effectively any game or activity in this book, be sure that you follow these guidelines:

1. Read the "Introduction" and "Guidelines for Success." Be sure to preset and close each activity.

2. Scan the activity overview and objectives to find one that suits your needs.

3. Select an activity; read the description and procedure thoroughly.

4. If the description says, "Small group or entire class," you may want to try it, if you can, with a small group at first. This will give you a trial run to identify and solve problems.

5. Walk through the activity with the class before putting it into full action. Demonstrate the activity first for the class.

6. Set clear ground rules. You may want to set a time limit.

7. If an activity calls for the class to guess what one student is performing or pantomiming, allow for only *three* attempts at guessing. If no one guesses what the student is doing, ask the student to tell the class. Then be sure he or she gets the same level of applause that the other students have received.

8. Talk quietly and slowly. Be patient. Encourage self-expression of the students. Avoid sarcasm or imposing your ideas. If you are not clear as to what a student is doing, ask them politely to explain. You may be pleasantly surprised by the answer.

9. Modify the activity to reinforce positively as many students as possible. Try to say something positive about every response.

10. After you use the activity, modify it to fit your own personal teaching style and the personality of your students.

Assess Your Own Success

After you use an activity in your class, evaluate the success of the lesson with this simple checklist.

1. Did you read the "Introduction" and "Guidelines for Success" thoroughly?
   ☐ Yes   ☐ No

2. Did you familiarize yourself with the activity you selected?
   ☐ Yes   ☐ No

3. Did you try the activity in a small group or walk through it with your class before using it on a full scale?
   ☐ Yes   ☐ No

4. Were you able to lead the activity by being the first participant?
   ☐ Yes   ☐ No

5. Did you set clear ground rules?
   ☐ Yes   ☐ No

6. Did you talk quietly and slowly?
   ☐ Yes   ☐ No

7. Did you preset and close the activity?
   ☐ Yes   ☐ No

8. Did you encourage creativity versus imposing your ideas?
   ☐ Yes   ☐ No

9. Did you positively reinforce as many students as possible?
   ☐ Yes   ☐ No

10. Did you praise your students and yourself for trying?
    ☐ Yes   ☐ No

2

Activities for Review and Reinforcement

The following section includes a variety of fun and uncomplicated games for classroom use. All of the activities may be used on an ongoing basis since they can easily be adapted for use across the curriculum. Note that many of these games are review tools. They are designed to supplement and extend lessons in which concepts have already been introduced. However, you will also find several games that can be used to introduce new material.

The activities throughout the book are described in detail in the Procedure & Dialogue sections. In the Procedure section, the strategy is spelled out in step-by-step fashion. Each dialogue entry corresponds with a procedural step to help you know what to say to students as you implement the activity.

Category List

Here is a list of some of the categories that can be used with many of the review games and activities found in this section. Of course, it is best to link these activities to themes, literature, or units already being studied. This list is simply provided to spark your imagination. Once you use these techniques you will see that the list is endless.

- Nouns, verbs, adjectives, adverbs, prepositions, conjunctions, compound words, transition words

- Words that start with a particular letter

- Colors shapes
- Types of animals
- Types of vegetables
- Types of fruits
- Primary numbers
- Odd numbers
- Even numbers
- Characters in a story
- Facts about dinosaurs, snakes, history—anything!
- Elements of a fairy tale, a myth, a tall tale
- Multiples of a number
- Modes of transportation
- Community helpers
- Jobs
- Toys
- Types of clothing
- Holidays
- States and their capitals
- Countries
- Seasons
- Types of cars
- Things found in:
  the living room
  the dining room
  the kitchen
  New York
  Washington
  Tokyo
  a city
  a farm . . .

Food Pantomime

Overview: Students pantomime eating various foods; an excellent first creative drama activity

Objective: To give students a basic definition of the words "pretend" and "imagination"
To give students a simple beginning creative drama experience

Grade level: PreK to 3

Materials: None

Group size: Entire class

Classroom setup: In circle or at desks

Procedure & Dialogue

1. Preset the class.

   '*Today we are going to pretend and use our imagination. So let's begin.*'

2. Ask the students to use their imagination and pretend to find in front of them an imaginary food. In this example, an ice cream cone is found.

   '*Reach out in front of you and grab an ice cream cone.*'

3. Keep the class together by asking them to show you the food.

   '*Hold it up. Let me see it. Oohh, it looks delicious. I have chocolate chip! What flavor do you have?*'

4. Take the students, step-by-step, through eating the food.

   '*We'd better eat our ice cream cone soon. What will happen if we don't? Right. It will melt. So let's eat it. Take one big slurp. Now another. Faster, faster, faster. Bite the bottom of the cone and suck all the ice cream from the bottom. Now chew the rest of your cone as fast as you can. Oh, that was delicious. Now grab a napkin and wipe your face and hands. Now put the napkin in the trash can next to you.*'

5. Then ask the students if they really ate an ice cream cone. Use the opportunity to define reality, pretending, and the imagination.

   '*Now that we have finished eating, I have something to ask you. Did we really eat an ice cream cone? Did we really wipe our face with a napkin? No! That's right. Do you remember what I said we were going to do? . . . pretend and use a special part of our brain—the imagination.'*

6. Close the activity.

'*Let's pretend again. Reach behind your ear, get a little magic dust, and at the count of three, let's throw it, and it will make everything we just pretended—the trash can, the napkin—disappear. One . . . two . . . three . . .'*

Modifications for Younger Students, PreK to K

1. You can add cold foods and hot foods as a way to explore contrasts.

'*We ate the ice cream very quickly. Oh, my throat is cold. Let's get something hot to drink. How about some hot chocolate? Reach out and find that hot chocolate —let me see it.'* (Continue step-by-step leading them through drinking the hot chocolate. Blow on it if it is too hot, put marshmallows or whipped cream on it, and so on.)

2. You can emphasize positional words.

'*Put the ice cream beside you. Put it behind you. Put it over your head.'*

3. You can extend the activity to review body parts and cleanliness.

'*Oh no! We have ice cream all over us. We have it on our _____ (point and have the children say the body part). We have it on our _____ (point). We'd better clean up. (Take them through those activities step-by-step). Let's turn on our sink right in front of us. Now be sure the water's not too hot. Now get your soap. Let me see it . . .'*

Comments

Peanut butter, french fries, and pizza are other good foods for this activity.

This activity is great for ESL students and students with language delay, who may not know the meaning of the words "pretend" and "imagination." It gives them an active experience with these words and sets the stage for future creative drama activities.

Personal Notes & Adaptations

Motion Sound Game One & Motion Sound Game Two

Overview: A memory and prewriting activity that uses motions (pantomime) and words simultaneously

Objective: To review various educational concepts

Grade level: PreK to 6

Materials: None

Group size: Small groups or entire class

Classroom Setup: No particular setup is required

Motion Sound Game One: Procedure & Dialogue

1. Select a topic for review. (See the Category List for ideas.) The topic here is action verbs.

   '*We talked about the action verbs we found in our story yesterday, and today we're going to learn more of them. I want everyone to choose one action verb. Feel free to choose one from the list we wrote on the board yesterday.*'

2. Present a motion as you say the verb. It is best if the motion reflects the meaning of the word.

   '*Now I want you to think of a motion that goes with the action verb that you have chosen. For instance, if I chose this verb, I might do this. Swim (pantomime the motion of swimming). Say and do "swim" with me now: "Swim" (do motion).*'

3. Have each student then present a word and a motion for their verb.

   '*Laura, you try it. What verb did you choose? Dance! Show us a motion for dance. Let's all do Laura's motion and say, "Dance".*'

4. Have the class repeat each verb and motion after it is presented. Then review the previous verbs and motions with the intent to memorize them all.

   '*Good, Beth. Now let's do Beth's verb and motion together. Now let's try to do everyone's right in order. Start with mine.*'

Modifications for Older Students

5. In grades 3 through 6, have the students develop the game further. After all the verbs have been presented and memorized, have Student A begin by doing his or her own motion and word and then call on Student B by imitating his or her motion and word. Student B then does his or her own motion and sound and calls on Student C, and so on.

   'Okay, Laura, say and do your verb, and now call on someone else by doing and saying theirs. Good. Now Jody, do your motion and verb and call on someone else by doing theirs.'

Alternative Ways to Play

1. Make the game a guessing game. Have the students write down the word or concept. Then have each pantomime a motion for the word and have a team or the rest of the class guess what he or she is doing. If the class does not guess after three attempts, have the student say and do the word he or she is presenting. (See the "Adjective Game.")

Motion Sound Game Two: Procedure & Dialogue

1. The same activity described in "Motion Sound Game One" can be used as a prewriting activity to motivate group or individual writing.

2. When using the game for this purpose, select a topic with which the students have some familiarity.

   'We just read an article about Dr. Martin Luther King, Jr.'

3. Feel free to add a critical-thinking component to the activity.

   'I want you to think of something you think the world should remember about Dr. King—a quality , a fact about his life—and then create a motion to go with your idea.'

4. Go first to set an example. Be sure your example sets the tone and expectations for the activity. Write the word or phrase on the board.

   'What I think the world should remember about Dr. Martin Luther King, Jr., is that he was nonviolent (pantomime a motion that reflects the concept)*.'*

5. Since this is a bit more difficult, you may want to have students work in pairs. Inform the students that it is all right to present a phrase rather than just one word.

'Work with a partner and come up with a word or phrase that tells us something you think the world should remember about Dr. Martin Luther King, Jr.'

6. Give them time to prepare.

   'Take a few minutes to get your ideas, and then rehearse them a few times.'

7. Have each group (student) present. Then write each idea on the board.

   'Matt and James, what did you come up with? Equal. Good, I'll put it on the board.'

8. Have the class repeat each motion and word (phrase).

   'Let's say and do it together. EQUAL (do motion).'

9. Get all who are willing and ready to present their ideas.

   'Patrice and Jenny, what do you have? I HAVE A DREAM. Oh! That's lovely. Let's say and do it together. I HAVE A DREAM (do motion).'

10. Once the students have generated their list, have them repeat each word (phrase) and motion.

    'Let's say and do them all.'

11. The entire class can work together to compose a paragraph using these words, or students can work in groups or individually to create sentences using these words.

    'I want you to work with your partners again and come up with a sentence that goes with your word.'

12. Write all the sentences on the board. Discuss with the students the order of the sentences.

13. Create more motions for words that lend themselves to illustration in this way.

    'What other words up here could we create motions for?'

14. Have the students use shared reading to read the paragraph aloud. Be sure they do all the motions as well.

    'Let's read our paragraph together and do all the motions we created.'

15. Feel free to have them reread it.

    'That was so wonderful. Let's do it one more time.'

16. Close the activity.

    '*You did a great job. Give yourself a hand.*'

17. This same structure can be used for a season, a historical event, or even a holiday.

    '*Winter is snowflakes fluttering to the ground* (do a motion). *What else is winter? Who can give me a sentence and a motion to go with it?*'

18. Students can also work in groups and then present their own sentences and motions.

19. After you've generated a list of words and/or ideas, students can do some critical thinking along with their writing.

    '*I want you to look at the list on the board and decide what three things you think are the most important. Then write and tell me why.*'

Comments

If students cannot think of a motion to go with their word or phrase, let several other students suggest a motion.

This is an excellent and endless review technique.

Personal Notes & Adaptations

Pass the Eraser

Overview: A fast-paced, timed memory and concentration game

Objective: To review various educational concepts

Grade level: K to 6

Materials: A box or coffee can, 3x5-inch index cards, a quiet object, *e.g.*, a clean eraser, hot pad, potato, or the like.

Group size: Small group or entire class

Classroom setup: A circle is best, but can be played with the students seated at their desks

Procedure & Dialogue

1. Place in a box or can the index cards with a set of instructions or questions written on them that you want to review. (See the Category List for ideas.) Students can also create their own questions.

2. If possible, place the students in a circle with Student A seated in the center.

3. Place in Student A's hands a small object, preferably one that makes no sound when it is passed. An eraser is used here.

4. Student A then closes his or her eyes and passes the eraser out to the circle or down the row of seats. The students pass the eraser as quickly and quietly as possible until Student A says, "Stop!" The person holding the eraser when "Stop!" is said is Student B.

    '*Ed, close your eyes and pass the eraser out to the circle. As soon as you get it, begin to pass the eraser as fast as you can around the circle. Ed, say "Stop!" whenever you are ready. Good. Marcie has the eraser.*'

5. Student A reaches into the can and then reads the question or set of instructions on the card. The topic here is nouns. Student B must then name five nouns by the time the eraser makes another complete pass around the circle. If five is too difficult, start with one. If five becomes easy, increase the number of items. For grades K–1, start with one.

    '*Ed, reach in the can, get a card and read the instructions. It says: Name five nouns.*'

6. Inform Student B that he or she must concentrate on the task of answering the question and not on the eraser moving around the circle. If Student B watches the eraser, he or she will not be able to complete the task. For those with concentration problems, have them close their eyes or look at the floor.

'*Remember, Marcie, to think of the nouns. Don't watch the eraser, or you won't be able to complete the instructions. Okay, pass the eraser around the circle.*'

7. Inform the students that if anyone shouts out or tries to help Student B find the answers, those answers will not count, and the student who helps will be denied a turn.

'*No one try to help Marcie. Johnny, that noun won't count, and you lost your chance to play on the next round.*'

8. If Student B does not accomplish this, he or she goes into the middle. The game then begins again.

'*Marcie named four. Let's give her a hand for that. Who can name one more noun? Excellent. Okay, Marcie, now come into the middle.*'

Alternative Ways to Play

9. If Student B does not complete the task, Student A must answer the question before being allowed to exit from the middle.

'*Ed, you now have to name five different nouns before the eraser comes back to Marcie in order to get out of the middle.*'

10. If students start to fail purposefully at the task in order to get into the middle, then just randomly select who goes into the middle.

11. In order to be sure all students are listening, get the students to repeat the five items Student B named before continuing with the game.

'*Okay, what four nouns did Marcie name? Who was listening? Let's write them on the board.*'

12. If Student B does not achieve the task and is upset by that, have Student B hold the object in his or her hands and name at least one item in the category.

'*Marcie, now that the pressure is off, can you name one more noun for us? Good. Let's give her a hand.*'

Activity Variations

1. This activity can be used for spelling review. Have the students spell a word correctly by the time the eraser goes around the circle.

2. This activity can also be used with math. Have the students solve a problem by the time the eraser goes around the circle.

3. The teacher can always be the person in the middle and provide all the questions. This allows the teacher to modify the questions on the spot in order to meet the needs of individual students. This increases the chances of student success.

4. When the game is played with students sitting at desks, it takes longer for the eraser to get around. Therefore, you may want to designate a place for the eraser to stop, instead of passing it to every student.

   'Sergio, I want you to answer the question by the time the eraser goes down these two aisles and gets to Paula.'

Comments

1. This is an active game; but keep in mind that learning is going on, and students are getting excited about remembering educational concepts.

2. Note all the control devices built into the game.

3. Students love to play this game. They can play it independently.

Personal Notes & Adaptations

Motion Stop!

Overview: A game combining motions and visuals as a means for reviewing various topics

Objective: To assess students' comprehension
To promote memory and concentration

Grade level: PreK to 3

Materials: Colored construction paper

Group size: Small groups or entire class

Classroom setup: At desks

Procedure & Dialogue

1. Choose a category to be reviewed. (See the Category List for ideas.) The topic here, for grades PreK–K, is numeral recognition.

2. Place on construction paper the numerals to be reviewed. Put one number on each piece of paper. Depending on the level of the students, you may or may not want to use the numerals out of sequence.

   'Let's review all the numbers up to ten in order. Now I'm going to mix them up. Let's see how you do. 1 . . . 5 . . . 7 . . .'

3. Select one number as the "Special Number of the Day." Explain that whenever the number appears, students must stop moving and be perfectly still. Please note: It is best to use only one or two colors of construction paper for this activity. If you use many colors, students may focus on the color of the special number rather than on recognizing the numeral.

   'Now what number is this? Right, number 9. Nine is our Special Number of the Day. Whenever you see the number 9, I want you to stop whatever you are doing.'

4. Introduce a motion for the class to do. Then show them the special number and get them to stop all action immediately.

   'Now I want you to tap your head. Keep tapping, but when we see the number 9, what are we going to do? Right! We're going to stop!'

5. Place the special number randomly among the other numbers. Select a motion for the class to perform, *e.g.,* tap their feet, clap, snap their fingers, or wiggle a finger.

'Okay, now I'm going to hide our special number in the pile and whenever it turns up, what do we do? Right! We stop!'

6. They must continue doing the motion while singing the numbers that they see. Have them sing each number on a tone going up the scale. As soon as the special number appears, they must stop. Really look over the class thoroughly to see that all stop. Try to make stopping a challenge and fun.

'Now everyone tap your nose, and let's sing the numbers we see. "5 . . . 5 . . . 5 . . . 6 . . . 6 . . . 6 . . . 2 . . . 2 . . . 2 . . . 9! Oh look what it is." What do we do? Right, we stop.'

7. Place the special number back in the pile, select another motion, and start again.

'Good. Let's hide it and start again. This time who has an idea for a motion we can do?'

Activity Variation for Older Students

1. In grades two to three, the concepts can be more difficult, *e.g.,* nouns, verbs, multiples of 3, contractions, adjectives, adverbs, or primary numbers. Instead of a special noun, verb, or whatever insert one or more items that are incorrect or that do not fit the category. For example, if all of the items are adjectives, insert several verbs randomly in the pack. The students then do their motions, and when they see the incorrect cards, they must immediately stop.

Another way to play is to have all the students stand up and when the incorrect answer appears, they must immediately sit down or vice versa.

Comments

Students love this game. Children in PreK–1 find it extremely amusing. See "Motion Now" for a modification of this activity.

Feel free to lead this game in role (see Chapter 6 "Role Play"). You could create a character who returns again and again to your classroom whenever you play this game.

Personal Notes & Adaptations

Motion Now!

Overview: A true-false game for the entire class using shared reading

Objective: To assess students' comprehension
To promote memory and concentration

Grade level: 1 to 6

Materials: Large drawing tablet or overhead projector

Group size: Entire class

Classroom setup: At desks

Procedure & Dialogue

1. On large pieces of paper (drawing tablets or transparencies can be used), write various facts about a book, an article, or a topic with which the students are familiar. Make some of the statements true and some of them false.

   'On these cards I have some statements about Washington, D.C. I want you to read these statements aloud together with me.'

2. Ask the class to read each statement together. Tell them to do one motion if the statement is true and a different motion if the statement is false.

   'If the statement is true, I want you to point to the ceiling. If the statement is false, give me the thumbs-down sign. Let's read it together.'

3. If the statement is false, have the class correct the statement.

   'You're telling me that this statement is not true. I see all your thumbs are down. How could I make this a true statement? Good. Now let's go on to the next sentence.'

4. You can change motions every two or three statements. Changing the motion extends listening skills.

   'Now if the next statement is true, I want you to clap one time. If it is false, scratch your head. Let's read together.'

Comments

This game gives you an instant assessment of what students have comprehended. It is a great activity for the opening of a lesson.

Use only eight to ten statements at a time. After that, students may lose interest.

You may want to move brighter students to the back of the room so that the other students do not look to them for their answers. However, if you do that you may want to randomly move other students as well, so the class does not suspect your motives.

At first, the students may be uncomfortable reading together. Keep encouraging them to do so. Shared reading helps all students to read and creates a sense of unity in the class.

If your students have low self-esteem, you may want to make the motions small and close to the body so that students do not have to risk making a choice that the entire class can see.

See "Motion Stop!" for a modification of this activity.

Feel free to lead this activity as a character (see Chapter 6, "Role Play"). You could create a character who returns whenever you do this activity.

For ESL Students

The use of shared reading in this activity is very helpful for ESL students.

If you work with small groups of ESL students, you may want to include more complicated motions. For instance, "If it is true, go and stand by the window. If it is false, put your hand on the blackboard." These directions give the students more receptive language experience.

Personal Notes & Adaptations

Name It!

Overview: A team game involving sets/classification

Objective: To review various classifications
To promote memory and spontaneity

Grade level: 2 to 6

Materials: Set of alphabet cards

Group size: Entire class

Classroom setup: In teams

Procedure & Dialogue

1. Divide the class into two or more teams.

2. Discuss with students the concept of sets/classification. Each team is then assigned or chooses a set. The sets may be anything on the Category List or more general categories, such as things that fly, dairy products, sports equipment, or items found in a home.

3. Mix up a set of alphabet cards. Randomly select one card from the pile. Show the letter to Team A. Team A then has to name one item from their set that begins with that letter in order to receive a point. Select another letter for Team B. An additional point may be added for writing the word on the chalkboard and spelling it correctly.

   'The letter is "Z." Sophia, name a noun that starts with "Z." Zebra, good. That gives Team A one point. Now Team B, the letter is "O." Name a noun that starts with "O."'

Activity Variations

1. Have the teams secretly choose their own set so that the other team(s) does not know what it is. The game is played the same way. The first team that can guess the set of the other team scores an additional 10 points.

2. For all students, including ESL students: Instead of the letters of the alphabet written on the flash cards, place a general category or the name of the person, place, or thing on the card. Each team member must then share one fact about the subject on the card. For instance, if the flash card said "Living Room," the student would name one object found in a living room. If the card said "Thomas Jefferson,"

the student would need to share one fact about Thomas Jefferson. In addition, the same card could be shown to both teams in order for the students to hear more than one fact about a topic.

Comments

This is another game that can be even more fun if the leader conducts the game in role (see Chapter 6, "Role Play"). Feel free to create a game show host who can return throughout the year. Once the students know this game they can lead this activity in or out of role themselves.

Personal Notes & Adaptations

Environment Orchestra

Overview: A game in which students identify and create the sounds found in a particular environment

Objective: To review elements of a particular environment and location

Grade level: PreK to 6

Materials: None

Group size: Small groups or entire class

Classroom setup: No particular setup needed

Procedure & Dialogue

1. Select one environment, *e.g.*, New York; Tokyo; Washington, D.C.; the zoo; a factory; a train station; an airport; a farm. The topic here is New York.

2. Have the class identify what sounds are part of that environment.

   '*What sounds would you hear in New York City? We would hear the harbor, taxis, horns, police whistles, people walking, and street vendors. Good.*'

3. Have the students recreate these sounds using their voices and their bodies.

   '*Who can make a sound like a boat in New York harbor? Let's all try that together. Can you do an action to go with that sound? Now who can make a taxi sound? Good. What action can you do? Let's try that.*'

4. Once five or six sounds have been identified and imitated, divide the class into groups. Give each group a sound.

   '*I want table one to be the harbor sounds. Let me see and hear you. Now table two, I want you to be street vendors.*'

5. Explain that the class will now become the orchestra, playing the symphony of this particular environment. You will conduct. Provide the class with motions for louder, softer, faster, slower, stop, and start. The conductor controls it all by the motions.

   '*You are now the orchestra playing the Symphony Number One of New York City. When I make this motion, I want you to begin. This means softer. This means louder. This means faster and this means slower. And this means stop. Orchestra, are you ready? Then let's begin.'*

Activity Variations

1. The students can be divided into groups beforehand, come up with their own environment, and create their own symphony; the class could then guess what environment was presented.

2. Emotions can also be explained in this way. Create a symphony for happiness, frustration, or anger.

3. The environment could be modified to be the inside of a character's (person's) mind. The students could identify the repeating thoughts of the characters (person) and create an orchestra of their brain.

Comments

A great review exercise for any environment or location being studied.

Personal Notes & Adaptations

Change Three

Overview: An observation game done in pairs

Objective: To strengthen observation skills and independent thinking

Grade level: PreK to 3

Materials: None

Group size: Small groups or entire class

Classroom setup: Clear space

Procedure & Dialogue

1. Break the students into pairs.

2. Have the students observe carefully everything their partner is wearing.

   'Look at your partner carefully. Look at everything he or she is wearing, the jewelry, and how his or her hair is combed.'

3. One partner, Player A, turns his or her back on the other, Player B.

   'Now one of you turn your back on your partner. We'll call you Player A.'

4. Player B then changes three things about his or her appearance. Stress subtlety. They can change anything from their clothing, their hair, or the way they are standing.

   'Now the other partner, Player B, I want you to change three things about the way you look. Be sneaky!'

5. When all changes have been completed, Player A turns around and tries to find the three things that have been changed.

6. Check to see who succeeded.

   'How many of you found all three things? Good!'

7. Switch, and let Player A change three things.

   'Now switch and all the letter A's will do the same thing. Really be tricky!'

8. The game can continue by having additional items changed on each round. Six items is a realistic goal.

Activity Variations

1. After the students have played the game and are familiar with it, use the structure of the game for other lessons. Have the students place stickers on their bodies with various parts of speech, for example, conjunctions. Have them observe each other, remove three, and see if their partners can identify which conjunctions have been removed.

2. Let the students put on costumes from a costume box to make the game more fun and challenging.

3. In grades PreK to 1, introduce the game by changing three things on you in the front of the room. Make the things you change very obvious so they understand the concept of the activity.

For ESL Students

This is a good activity for beginning level ESL students to help them develop vocabulary pertaining to clothing.

Comments

Students love this game.

Personal Notes & Adaptations

Shape Game

Overview: Students must stand on a shape placed on the floor to indicate an appropriate response.

Objective: To review various concepts through a physical response.

Grade level: PreK to 4

Materials: Multicolored fabric shapes

Group size: Small group or entire class

Classroom setup: Semicircle with students on the floor or in chairs; a carpeted space is ideal

Procedure & Dialogue
For Students, PreK–K

1. Place colored shapes on the floor.

2. Ask the students to jump or hop to a particular shape and/or color.

   'Cheryl, I want you to jump to the orange square. Now jump to the blue circle.'

3. After instructing the students to jump or hop to several locations, ask them to tell you where they are going to jump to next.

   'Now Cheryl, tell me where would you like to jump?'

Optional

4. Create a puppet or a character who knows less than the students (see "Role Play, Lesson One"). Have the students pick up the shapes as they teach shapes and/or colors to the character or puppet. Here, a puppet is used. Be sure to tell the students what to expect.

   'You know what: I have a little friend who lives in this can. Her name is Sunny, and she doesn't know her shapes and colors. She's crying. Can you hear her crying? Will you teach her her shapes and colors? Let's ask Sunny to come out. Let's tell Sunny we'll help her.'

5. When using a puppet, as in role play, turn your back to the students as you put the puppet on your hand. When you

face the class, become the voice and character of the puppet. Keep the puppet in front of your face and the eyes of
the puppet at eye level of the student(s).

'(As Sunny) *Whaaaa! Whaaaa! All the kids in my class
know their colors and shapes except me. Will you help
me? You will! Great! Nicole, will you pick up a shape and
color and teach it to me? What is that Nicole? It's a red
circle?*'

6. To promote more language, ask the student to verify the
answer.

'*Nicole, ask Tanya if that's a red circle.*'

7. If the student teaches the puppet the wrong answer, you
can use other students as class experts to correct the
response.

'*Nicole, Tanya says that's an orange circle. Ask Michael.
Michael says it's an orange circle. Guess what Nicole? I
think it's an orange circle. What color is it Nicole? Right,
orange!*'

8. Reward the students. If a student doesn't want a kiss as a
reward, don't force him or her to take one. Offer a hand-
shake or just a big thank you instead.

'*Nicole, can I give you a kiss for teaching me orange circle?
Tanya and Michael can I give you a kiss too for helping me?*'

9. Continue working with the other students.

'*Now who else will teach me a color and a shape?*'

10. This puppet or character can be used for any topic.
Students are eager to help anyone who knows less than
they do.

Modifications for Older Students, Grades 1–4

1. Put answers to math problems on multicolored shapes on
the floor. (Use fabric paint or large stick-on labels.)

'*On the floor you see multiples of six.*'

2. Show a card with a math problem on it that matches one of
the answers on the floor. Ask the student to stand on the
answer to the problem.

'On these cards are problems that equal the answers you see on the floor. I'm going to hold up a problem; we will read it together, and then I will call on someone to go and stand on the answer. Here's the first card. Let's read it. $6 \times 6 = ?$ Who knows the answer and will go and stand on it?'

3. Instead of students standing or jumping on a shape, they can move a toy to the appropriate answer. For instance, you might want to have students place Wanda, the Wise Old Owl, on the right answer, or Jimmy, the Jumping Frog.

4. Another option is to use a hat or a costume piece to turn the students into a character who is searching for the right answer such as Waldo, the Wise Old Wizard, or Denise, the Daring Detective (see "Role Play"). These devices help to focus and motivate students.

Activity Variations

1. The game is endless in its uses. Younger students can jump or stand on numerals, letters, words that have a particular consonant or vowel sound, and so on.

2. Older students can use the game for vocabulary development as well. The cards can have a word on them, and the definitions could be on the floor or vice versa.

For ESL Students

The students can match a picture to a word on the floor.

Personal Notes & Adaptations

Magic Box/Magic Hat

Overview: Students visualize and utilize an imaginary box that can contain anything from a verb to a dream come true.

Objectives: To review various educational concepts
To stimulate independent and creative thinking

Grade level: PreK to 6

Materials: None (a real box optional for PreK to 1, ESL students, or students who are mentally challenged)

Group size: Small group or entire class

Classroom setup: A circle or at desks; put a desk or table at the front of room

Magic Box:
Procedure & Dialogue

1. Decide what you would like to put in the box for the students to find. The uses for the box are endless. (See the Category List for ideas.)

2. Preset the class.

   'Today we're going to pretend and use our imaginations. So let's begin.'

3. Relaxation.

   'I want you to close your eyes.'

4. Have the students visualize a magic box in the front of the room.

   'When you open your eyes at the count of three, you will see —if you are using your imagination— a magic box on the desk in the front of the room. Ready? One ... two ... three ...'

5. Show them the box through pantomime, and discuss the properties of the box, such as color, size, and texture. Discuss the writing on the box. Accept all answers as correct. If a student denies seeing the box, respond with, "You're right, you'll only see the box if you use your imagination" (see "Guidelines for Success").

   'Here it is! Who sees my imaginary box? Good. What color is my box? Pink—yes, there's a pink stripe. What other color is it? Orange with purple polka dots—yes, there are the polka dots right there! What does it say on the box?'

6. Pantomime opening the box. Tell the class what you've placed inside the box.

'Now I'm going to open the box, and I'll tell you what's inside. In the Magic Box today is a present for the Earth. We have been studying ways to save the Earth, and in this box are gifts we can give the Earth in order to save it. Each of you will find something and pantomime using it, and the class will try to guess what it is. I'll go first to show you what I mean.'

7. Demonstrate what you want them to do. Reach in the box, find the object, and have the class guess what you found. Pantomime using the object.

'Can anyone guess what I'm doing? That's right. I'm turning off lights to save energy.'

8. Select a student to follow the same process. Bring students up one by one. If the class is large, you can do half the class one day and the other half the next.

'Who would like to go next? Reach in the box.'

9. Give the class three times to try and guess the object found. If no one guesses, have the student explain.

'Joel, reach in and find a gift for the Earth. Show it to us, but don't tell us what it is. Who can guess? Laura, what do you think it was? Who else can guess? Amy? Ken? What do you think it was? We don't know. Tell us, Joel. Oh, great! He was picking up all the litter off the streets.'

10. Applaud each student.

'Let's give Joel a hand. Who's next?'

11. Close the activity.

'Now I want you to close your eyes and at the count of three, the Magic Box will be gone. It will have disappeared, and there will be a clean desk at the front of the room. One . . . two . . . three . . .'

Alternative Ways to Play

For a class needing more structure, simply have students visualize their own boxes under their chairs at their desks. They can share what they found right at their seats.

Activity Variations

1. "Magic Box" can be used to review anything. Objects can be placed in the box that have a certain beginning consonant sound or vowel sound. The possibilities are endless.

Magic Hat:
Procedure & Dialogue

1. "Magic Hat" begins the same way. Follow steps 2 to 6 of "Magic Box." Place in the box a magic hat capable of turning the students into somebody else, perhaps someone they've always wanted to be. It could be an animal, character from a story, or even someone they admire or would like to be. This activity is a simple form of role play (see Chapter 6, "Role Play").

2. Demonstrate how the hat works:

   a. Hold the hat over your head.

   b. Close your eyes and think of something you'd like to turn into.

   c. Put the hat on.

   d. Have the class count to three.

   e. Open your eyes, and become someone or something else.

   f. You may need to move and sound differently than you usually do.

   'Ahh! Hello boys and girls. My name is Farmer Jones. Your teacher asked me to come here today to talk to you about plants and what they need to grow and to tell you about my farm. On my farm I grow . . .'

3. After a minute or two, remove the hat. Have students identify your real name and who you pretended to be.

   '(Take off hat.) Oh, my goodness. Who am I really? And who did I turn into?'

4. Select students, one by one, to follow the same process. You hold the hat, place it, and remove it as a control device. Encourage students not to turn into television or movie characters. If they do, remove the hat and try again.

   'Who would like to come up and turn into something or somebody else we might find on the farm? Remember— you can't turn into anyone from television or movies.'

5. Interview the character (see "Role Play, Lesson Three"). Feel free to use the imaginary microphone (see "Guidelines for Success").

   'Welcome to our class. And what is your name please? What would you like to tell us about yourself?'

6. Follow steps 10 and 11 of "Magic Box."

Activity Variations

1. "Magic Hat" can be structured so that the students transform into any type of character, *e.g.*, animals, community helpers, insects, or even world leaders.

2. Using "Role Play, Lesson Three" in connection with "Magic Hat" can lead to storybuilding and oral and written composition.

3. "Imaginary Mask" is a good extension activity for "Magic Hat."

Comments

Teachers have used Magic Box as an ongoing activity in the classroom. Some store the imaginary box on a shelf or in a closet. Keep in mind if you do this the students *never* forget where you put it; so put it high up and out of reach.

This activity develops peer cooperation and respect. Students like to see and guess what other students discover in the box.

Personal Notes & Adaptations

Imaginary Door

Overview: Students draw an imaginary door and find a myriad of things behind it

Objective: To review or reinforce concepts
To build vocabulary

Grade level: PreK to 6

Materials: None

Group size: Entire class

Classroom setup: At desks or in circle

Procedure & Dialogue

1. Preset the class.

   '*Today we are going to use our imaginations and find a door right in front of us.*'

2. Have the students draw a door in front of them with a piece of imaginary chalk. The door can be a closet door in order to review clothing we need for a particular season, or it could be a door to any location the class may be studying. It could simply be a door to the future in preparation for a creative writing assignment. Here the door is a refrigerator door for a lesson about good food for grades PreK to 1. Please note: This lesson could be used as an extension to "Role Play, Lesson One."

   '*So reach beside you and find a piece of chalk. Let me see your chalk. Now today we are going to draw a refrigerator door. Let's go up one side of the door, across the top, and down the other side and across the bottom.*'

3. Tell them what they are going to see when they open the door.

   '*Now when we open the door we are going to find good food from one of the food groups we have been studying. We won't find anything with a lot of sugar. So let's open the door, reach in, and find some good food.*'

4. Have the students share what they've found.

   '*Who will share with me the good food you found in your refrigerator?*'

5. Close the activity.

'Now let's pick up our eraser and erase up one side, across the top, down the other side, and across the bottom. Now take some magic dust from behind your ear and, at the count of three, we will put it on our chalk and eraser, and they will disappear. Ready? One . . . two . . . three . . . Good. Now they have all disappeared and we are ready to . . .'

Comments and Modifications

The drawing of the door is an excellent focusing technique. It helps students relax and concentrate. It can be used in many ways to help active students focus their energies.

Behind the door could be something a character may have owned in a story the class has read, a crop of a particular country, a famous person from a particular country or historical period . . . the options are limitless.

For older students the magic dust is not needed at the end. Simply tell the students that at the count of three the chalk, door, and eraser will disappear.

For ESL Students

This activity is a great way to review the clothes that are worn in a particular season or things we might find in a room of a house or in a particular place.

Personal Notes & Adaptations

3

Strategies for Grammar & Spelling

 The ABC Game

Overview: A simple alphabet game

Objective: To review a variety of concepts
To develop concentration and spontaneity

Grade level: 1 to 6

Materials: None

Group size: Entire class

Classroom setup: No particular setup needed

Procedure & Dialogue

1. Select a topic for review (see the Category List for ideas).
   The topic here is nouns.

   '*What is a noun? Let's see how many we can name.*'

2. Start with the letter A.

   '*Who can name a noun that begins with A?*'

3. Get one to three answers, and move on through the entire
   alphabet.

   '*Who can name a noun that begins with B? C? D? . . .*'

Comments

You may want to do five to ten letters a day as an opening activity. The students will tire of the game if it doesn't move quickly. As a quick review, some teachers get just one example for each letter and move on.

This activity challenges and focuses students and is easy to use again and again with different subject matter.

Feel free to create a continuous character who leads this activity (see Chapter 6, "Role Play").

Personal Notes & Adaptations

3

Strategies for Grammar & Spelling

The ABC Game

Overview: A simple alphabet game

Objective: To review a variety of concepts
To develop concentration and spontaneity

Grade level: 1 to 6

Materials: None

Group size: Entire class

Classroom setup: No particular setup needed

Procedure & Dialogue

1. Select a topic for review (see the Category List for ideas).
   The topic here is nouns.

   '*What is a noun? Let's see how many we can name.*'

2. Start with the letter A.

   '*Who can name a noun that begins with A?*'

3. Get one to three answers, and move on through the entire
   alphabet.

   '*Who can name a noun that begins with B? C? D? . . .*'

Comments

You may want to do five to ten letters a day as an opening activity. The students will tire of the game if it doesn't move quickly. As a quick review, some teachers get just one example for each letter and move on.

This activity challenges and focuses students and is easy to use again and again with different subject matter.

Feel free to create a continuous character who leads this activity (see Chapter 6, "Role Play").

Personal Notes & Adaptations

Spell It!

Overview: A pantomime spelling game

Objective: To enhance spelling skills

Grade level: 2 to 6

Materials: Flash cards, chalk, chalkboard

Group size: Entire class

Classroom setup: At desks

Procedure & Dialogue

1. Put spelling words on index cards.

2. Select one student to begin. Have that student choose one card and then pantomime an action or an object for each letter of the word being spelled. Once the student begins to pantomime, he or she cannot talk until the word is correctly spelled.

   'In this spelling game, I want you to pantomime or act out an action for each letter of the word. So if the word was "crowd," you might act out driving a car for the first letter C; then running for the second letter R; you might open an imaginary box for the letter O; you could wave at the class for the letter W; or pretend to drop something for the last letter D.'

3. A recorder writes each letter on the board as the class guesses the letters.

4. If a student guesses the word before the acting-out process is completed, he or she can make a guess by completing the word and spelling it correctly on the chalkboard. Allow only one guess after each letter is discovered.

   'Alice, you think you know what the word is? Okay, take the chalk from the recorder and complete the word, but you must spell it correctly. That isn't the word, so let's see Tommy act out the next letter.'

5. This can be a team game like charades or a whole class activity.

6. For older students, if you use a point system, extra points can be given for defining the word correctly.

Alternate Ways to Play

1. Instead of one student acting out the word, make this a group activity. Give each group a word to act out and have the rest of the class guess the letters and the word.

2. To make the game more difficult, the letters of the word could be pantomimed out of sequence so that the class has to unscramble the letters as well.

Comments

1. This game is easier to understand if you show them the activity first.

2. The activity can also be done in pairs.

Personal Notes & Adaptations

Adjective Game/Adjective Charades/Vivid Verb Game

Overview: A team game involving adjectives or verbs

Objective: To promote vocabulary development
To promote concentration

Grade level: 2 to 6

Materials: Vary

Group size: Entire class

Classroom setup: In teams, at desks

Procedure & Dialogue

1. Divide the class into two teams.

2. A sentence without adjectives is placed on the board. Each team must supply a different adjective before every appropriate word in order to score a point.

   '*Johnny, I want you to put an adjective in the appropriate place in this sentence:* A bus and a truck had an accident near the playground. *Now we'll switch to the other team. Mary, I want you to put a different adjective in front of each appropriate word in the same sentence.*'

3. The same sentence can be used many times. This forces the students to search for new adjectives. A point is given for each successful turn by a player. You could also give each team a different sentence instead of using the same one for both teams.

   '*Let's keep the same sentence and do it again with different adjectives.*'

Adjective Charades

The same format is used, but instead of naming the adjective in the sentence, the team member must pantomime or act out the adjective. The team gets a point if the player can communicate each adjective to the team through his or her actions. They must write down their adjective secretly prior to acting it out.

The Vivid Verb Game

Follow the same steps as in the Adjective Game, but have the students supply vivid verbs for a simple sentence such as: The cat _____ out of the house. See how many verbs they can act out to fill in the blank. This can also be a guessing game. If it is a guessing game, be sure the students write down their verb secretly on a card prior to acting it out.

If you play this as a team game, you may want to give each team one sentence with which to work.

Personal Notes & Adaptations

The Punctuation Game

Overview: Students make a motion and sound for each punctuation mark. The game was inspired by Victor Borge's comedy routine on punctuation

Objective: To reinforce correct punctuation usage

Grade level: 2 to 6

Materials: Chalkboard and sentence strips

Group size: Small groups or entire class

Classroom setup: At desks or in groups

Procedure & Dialogue

1. Select various sounds to go with each punctuation mark you plan to introduce. Have the students repeat each sound and draw in the air with their finger that punctuation mark.

   '*Today we are going to put a sound and a motion with each of these punctuation marks. Let's say them together and draw the punctuation mark in the air with our finger as we say them:*

   > *A period is: pt*
   > *A comma is: neep*
   > *An apostrophe is: zt*
   > *A question mark is: ooo pt*
   > *An exclamation mark is: ft pt*
   > (Teachers: feel free to make up your own and add to the list.)'

2. Then have the students supply the missing punctuation marks in a sentence. Ask them to say the sound and do the motion for each of the missing punctuation marks.

   '*Look at this sentence:* Robins geese and herons are birds that migrate *Now let's add the punctuation that is missing. Read the sentence with me and add the motion and sound for each punctuation mark we need. Robins, (neep) geese, (neep) and herons are birds that migrate. (pt)*'

Modifications

This can be done as an entire class or as group work. Each group gets one sentence and then presents the corrected sentence to the class using the motions and sounds. After the group presents, be sure to have the entire class repeat the corrected sentence together using the motions and sounds. This keeps the class focused and on task.

Comments

Only introduce a few punctuation marks at a time.

A second-grade teacher in a school with many low-achieving students used this game on and off for two weeks with her class at the beginning of the year. A schoolwide oral reading test was given, and this second-grade class was not only one of the few classes to pass the test, but passed with some of the highest scores.

Personal Notes & Adaptations

Grandmother's Trunk (A Variation of "Magic Box")

Overview: Students fill an imaginary trunk with items needed for a long journey

Objectives: To promote memory and sequencing skills
To stimulate creative and independent thinking

Grade level: PreK to 3 (good for ESL students)

Materials: None (a real box or trunk optional)

Group size: Small groups or entire class

Classroom setup: A circle or at desks, a desk or table at the front of the room

Procedure & Dialogue

1. This game is similar to "Magic Box." In this game, students close their eyes and imagine they are all related and that their grandmother is going on a trip. Instead of taking objects out of the box, each student puts into her trunk a gift for Grandmother to use on her trip.

2. Read "Magic Box" and modify steps 2 through 5 to match description above.

3. After the class has visualized becoming a family and described the trunk, demonstrate, through pantomime, an object you are placing in the trunk for Grandmother.

   'Let's imagine then that we are one big family and our grandmother is going on a trip to Alaska. I'd like everyone to think of a gift we can give her and place in her trunk. But instead of telling us what it is, I'd like you to show it to us by pantomiming how you would use the object.'

4. Give the class three chances to try to guess the object.

   'Who can guess what I am putting in the trunk. Right! A shawl.'

5. Introduce the memory component of the game. Students are to recall and recite all the presents, once they've been identified, that are being given to Grandmother. The class can do this in unison, or each student can try to recite the list. If remembering all the items is too difficult, have the students remember five or six objects and then start again.

'Now after each person's object is guessed, we say "Grandmother's going to Alaska and in her trunk we put _____." We have to remember in order everything we put in the trunk. Let's try it. "Grandmother's going to Alaska and in her trunk we put a shawl, a camera, a bathrobe . . ."'

6. Go around the circle or up and down rows and have each student pantomime an object and place it in the trunk. Once it's identified, recite the entire list of objects in the trunk.

7. Close the activity.

'Close your eyes and at the count of three we will no longer be a family and our trunk will have disappeared. One . . . two . . . three . . .'

Activity Variations

1. Change the location to a place being studied or to reflect various seasons. For a hospital unit (Grades PreK-K), Grandmother could fill her suitcase with things she'll need for a hospital stay, or the class could fill a doctor's bag with what he or she needs for work.

2. This activity can be used with repeating beginning sounds, e.g. "Barbie goes to Baltimore." All objects have to begin with B.

3. This activity can be modified so that each object must have one or two adjectives in front of it that start with the same letter as the object, i.e., a soft silky scarf. You can add one or more adjectives each time you play the game.

4. This activity can be used with classification, e.g., fruits, colors, animals, shapes, sizes, or environments.

5. Students could place objects in the trunk in alphabetical order. The first student puts in an object that starts with A, the next student B, and so forth.

6. Combine this activity with "Imaginary Letter." Have the students write a letter to Grandmother.

7. Use the Magic Hat (see "Magic Hat") to turn a student into Grandmother, and interview her as to the nature and purpose of her trip (see "Role Play, Lesson Three").

8. Use the same structure for any recipe you might be making (see "Pizza/Submarine Sandwich/Picnic").

   '*We're making a salad, and in it we put tomatoes. Leslie, add something else to our salad. We're making a salad and in it we put tomatoes and cucumbers . . .*'

Comments

By dropping the pantomime component, the game can be modified for long car trips.

Personal Notes & Adaptations

Classifying & Sequencing Techniques

S ide by Side One & ■■ Side by Side Two

Overview: A matching game

Objective: To identify related concepts

Grade level: PreK to 6

Materials: Word cards or pictures

Group size: Small group or entire class

Classroom setup: Clear area for students to move

Side by Side One: Procedure & Dialogue

1. On large index cards, create a matched set of items. For instance, an inventor's name would be on one card and his or her invention would be on another card. In this example, the topic is states and their capitals.

   ‘*Today we are going to review states and their capitals.*’

2. Mix the cards up and randomly pass them out to half the class. Have the students look at their cards but not show them to anyone else until you say "Go!"

   ‘*Take one of these cards. Look at it, but do not let anyone else see it until I say, "Go!"*’

3. When you say "Go!" have the students show their cards and hold them in front of them. They cannot talk. They must silently look at the other cards and find their partner. They must find someone with a card that relates to the card they hold. Once they find their partner, they must stand side by side with that person.

   '*Go! Now show your cards. Hold them in front of you. Do not talk! See who is holding a card that goes with yours. When you find your partner, stand right next to them, side by side.*'

4. Once all the students are paired off have the rest of the class check for accuracy.

   '*Now everyone else look around. Has everyone matched the state with their capital? Challenge any pair you think may be wrong and ask them to defend their answer. It does look like everyone did a great job. Let's give them a hand.*'

5. Then reverse the game and have those that watched play the game.

   '*Now you sit down and we'll give the other students a turn.*'

Modifications

For matched sets that involve critical thinking or for students who need more opportunities to verbalize, have the students who pair up explain why they are together. Have them explain how the two concepts relate. Ask them to defend their answers.

For younger children or ESL students, pictures or a combination of pictures and words can be used.

Side by Side Two: Procedure & Dialogue

1. Use only six to eight students at a time for this activity. The game follows the same basic structure found in steps 1 and 2 above; however, when the leader says "Go!" the students must *not* show their cards. Instead they must silently act out what was on their card. Here the topic is compound words.

   '*Now look at your cards. Each card has part of a compound word on it. Now put your card face down on your desk. When I say "Go!" I want you to act out your word. You must do this silently.*'

Classifying & Sequencing Techniques

Side by Side One & Side by Side Two

Overview: A matching game

Objective: To identify related concepts

Grade level: PreK to 6

Materials: Word cards or pictures

Group size: Small group or entire class

Classroom setup: Clear area for students to move

Side by Side One: Procedure & Dialogue

1. On large index cards, create a matched set of items. For instance, an inventor's name would be on one card and his or her invention would be on another card. In this example, the topic is states and their capitals.

   '*Today we are going to review states and their capitals.*'

2. Mix the cards up and randomly pass them out to half the class. Have the students look at their cards but not show them to anyone else until you say "Go!"

   '*Take one of these cards. Look at it, but do not let anyone else see it until I say, "Go!"*'

3. When you say "Go!" have the students show their cards and hold them in front of them. They cannot talk. They must silently look at the other cards and find their partner. They must find someone with a card that relates to the card they hold. Once they find their partner, they must stand side by side with that person.

    'Go! Now show your cards. Hold them in front of you. Do not talk! See who is holding a card that goes with yours. When you find your partner, stand right next to them, side by side.'

4. Once all the students are paired off have the rest of the class check for accuracy.

    'Now everyone else look around. Has everyone matched the state with their capital? Challenge any pair you think may be wrong and ask them to defend their answer. It does look like everyone did a great job. Let's give them a hand.'

5. Then reverse the game and have those that watched play the game.

    'Now you sit down and we'll give the other students a turn.'

Modifications

For matched sets that involve critical thinking or for students who need more opportunities to verbalize, have the students who pair up explain why they are together. Have them explain how the two concepts relate. Ask them to defend their answers.

For younger children or ESL students, pictures or a combination of pictures and words can be used.

Side by Side Two: Procedure & Dialogue

1. Use only six to eight students at a time for this activity. The game follows the same basic structure found in steps 1 and 2 above; however, when the leader says "Go!" the students must *not* show their cards. Instead they must silently act out what was on their card. Here the topic is compound words.

    'Now look at your cards. Each card has part of a compound word on it. Now put your card face down on your desk. When I say "Go!" I want you to act out your word. You must do this silently.'

2. As the students act out their words, they must try to find their partners and stand side by side with them.

'Go! Now walk around the room, and keep acting out your word. See if you see someone who you think is the other half of your word. When you find that person, do not say anything but stand next to them—side by side.'

3. After all the students have found their partners, have them whisper their words to each other to see if they are correct. If not, have them move and try again.

'Once you think you have found your partner, whisper your word in your partner's ear. If you are not a matched set, move on and keep acting out your word until you find a new partner.'

4. Once all the partners have found each other, have each pair present their actions to the class and have the class guess what word or concept is being presented.

'Watch carefully, class. Erin is smearing something on bread and eating it and Bernice is flying around. What compound word do you think they are presenting? Right, butterfly.'

5. Then reverse the game and have those that watched play the game.

Comments

This game can be a lot of fun and stimulate a lot of creativity.

Sometimes I let the students use sounds in this activity but no words.

Personal Notes & Adaptations

Scramble Unscramble

Overview: Students unscramble cards or objects and put them in their proper sequence

Objective: To develop memory and sequencing skills
To develop classifying and organizing skills
To enhance concentration skills

Grade level: K to 6

Materials: Vary

Group size: Any size, a good group work activity

Classroom setup: No particular setup is necessary

Procedure & Dialogue

1. Give a group of students a set of cards or objects that reflect a sequence. Mix the cards up well so the sequence is scrambled.

   '*On your desk is a set of cards. On each card is a math problem.*'

2. Have the students unscramble the cards or objects and place them in their proper order.

   '*I want you to write the answer to the problem on the card and then put your answers in order on your desks starting with the lowest answer and moving on to the highest. You may begin—now!*'

Modifications

You may want to make this a timed activity.

You may want to make this a competitive activity in which the first group to unscramble the cards correctly wins a prize. If I do give a small prize, I often give something else to the whole class as well in recognition of their effort. I find students can become resentful otherwise.

For older students, you can expand and expand on this activity. You can have the students finish one unscrambling activity and then have each group pass their sets of cards on to another group or have the students create their own set of cards for another group.

For all students, including ESL students, sentence and paragraph structure, punctuation, math, days of the week, months of the year, words and their definitions can all be reinforced through this activity.

For younger students, pictures or objects can be used.

Comments

If done as a group activity, this game stimulates peer learning, language, and thinking skills.

For a sixth-grade group I combined "Scramble Unscramble" with the "Motion Sound Game." First I had the students unscramble a set of vocabulary words and their definitions for an article they were about to read. Then they had to say the words and act out the definitions of the words. It was very effective.

Again, feel free to facilitate this game as a character (see Chapter Six, "Role Play").

Personal Notes & Adaptations

Living Web, Lesson 1

Overview: Takes webbing or mapping off the page and brings it to life in front of the classroom

Objective: To promote organizing and classifying skills
To promote thinking skills

Grade level: PreK to 6

Materials: Vary

Group size: Small group or entire class

Classroom setup: In chairs at desks with a clear space at the front of the room

Procedure & Dialogue

1. Create signs out of posterboard. Attach to the signs strings or ribbons that dangle from various places along the edge of the sign. (See illustration in margin.)

2. The signs should reflect two or more contrasting categories. For instance, for younger students one sign may say "Fruits" and another may say "Vegetables." In the example here for intermediate-level students, one sign says "Action Verbs," another says "Linking Verbs," another says "Proper Nouns," and still another says "Common Nouns." (It is best if your topic is linked to a unit of study or a book or story with which the students are familiar.)

   '*After reading our story yesterday, we identified the action verbs, linking verbs, and common nouns and proper nouns in the story. Today we will be comparing action verbs, linking verbs, common nouns, and proper nouns. We'll be doing that through an activity called "Living Web."*'

3. Ask several students to hold up the large posterboard signs. The category should be written on the sign. Pictures can also be used.

   '*I need four students to hold up these signs. Good. Now spread out across the front of the room. The first sign says, "Action Verbs." The second says, "Linking Verbs" . . .*'

4. Other students select an index card with a word written on it; a picture or an object can also be used. The student must look at the word, picture, or object and decide to which category it belongs.

'Now I need a student to pick one of my cards. Ben, would you pick a card? What does it say? Think about that word, Ben: "walk." What kind of word is it? Is it an action verb, a linking verb, a common noun, or a proper noun? Go and stand where you think you belong and hold a string off that sign.'

5. Then the student walks over to the large sign that says the correct category and takes one of the strings.

   'Ben took the string of the category "Action Verbs."'

6. Sometimes words or objects can web more than once. This helps students understand more complex relationships.

   'Is he correct? Yes, he is, but what else can the word "walk" be besides an action verb? Right! "Walk" can also be a common noun. We can go for a "walk." So he needs to web twice. He needs to hold a string for the category "Action Verb" and another string for the category "Common Noun." Good. Who will go next?'

Activity Variations

Reverse the web. Give the students the cards with the supporting ideas and have them decide what is the main category. Then they can create the appropriate sign.

Modifications

Have half the class participate and the other half observe. Then reverse roles.

In order for the class to see all the relationships of the web clearly, I sometimes use an imaginary camera to "take a picture of the web" when the activity is completed. By "taking a picture," I elevate attention and get the students holding the web to hold it straight so that the visual image for the rest of the students is clear. (You can also use a real camera.)

For younger students or ESL students, pictures and/or small objects work best.

If your class is small or the children have short attention spans, put the webs on the floor.

Personal Notes & Adaptations

Living Web, Lesson 2

Overview: The game takes webbing or mapping off the page and brings it to life in front of the classroom

Objective: To promote classifying and thinking skills through a physical response

Grade level: 2 to 6

Materials: Signs (see "Living Web, Lesson One")

Group size: Small group or entire class

Classroom setup: Clear space at the front of the room and/or space for students to work in groups

Procedure & Dialogue

1. Do the activities "Statues One and Two" with your students before doing this lesson.

2. Read "Living Web, Lesson One" before doing this game.

3. Add a loop to the webbing signs so that the sign can fit around a student's neck (see "Living Web, Lesson One").

4. Break the class into groups, and give each group a sign. (For this activity you should have enough strings coming off the signs for each student in a group, or don't use strings at all.) Write on the sign a category with which the children are familiar. This might be from a thematic unit of study or from literature.

   'We just finished reading about bears, foxes, and wolves and where they live. Today we are going to do some group work based on what we've learned. Group I take this sign. Your group is going to focus on: "Shelters for Animals (Places Animals Live and Find Protection)." Group II, here is your sign. It says: "Shelters for Humans (Places Humans Live and Find Protection)." Group III, your sign says: "Animal Habitats."'

5. Instruct the students to generate a list of terms that fit these categories. They should try to have one term for each member of their group. Each student then takes the word or phrase and creates an action with his or her body that demonstrates this concept (see "Motion Sound" and "Statues One and Two").

'What I want you to do in your groups is to generate a list of words that apply to your category. For instance, one shelter for an animal might be a hole in a tree trunk. Then create a motion or an action that demonstrates this idea like this. (Show the action and say the word.) Then you will hold your pose like a statue until all your group members have presented their action. Generate enough ideas so that each group member can present.'

6. Invite the groups to the front of the classroom. Have one member of the group wear the sign and explain the category that is to be presented. Then one by one each group member does his or her action and says his or her word or phrase. Each student freezes and holds a pose of that motion (see "Statues One and Two") until the entire group has presented. (You may or may not want them to take a string from the main category sign as they present their actions.)

'Group II, will you start us off? Amber, please put the sign around your neck so we can all see what your group is doing. Tell us Amber, what is your topic? Great. Now, one by one present your actions and say your ideas, but hold the pose of your action by looking at a particular spot in the room until your whole group has presented. We want to see a sculpture of "Shelters for Humans." Good. Please begin.'

7. You may need to let the first few groups present a second time in order to eliminate giggling and uncomfortable feelings and so that you can get the strong visual image this activity can provide. Feel free to take an imaginary or real picture of the webs once they are completed (see "Living Web, Lesson One").

'That was great. Let's do that one more time now so we can really see the whole picture.'

Activity Variations for Older Students

1. Have them create a main category on their own and the supporting ideas.

2. Have the groups present only the supporting ideas, and have the class guess what the main category might be.

3. This could also be done as a guessing game in which the students take their poses and the class guesses what is being presented.

Comments

You may want the student who places the sign around his or her neck to also do an action, or you may want to save that job for a quiet student who may be hesitant to act in front of the class.

Personal Notes & Adaptations

Living Map/Living Time Line

Overview: Students create living sculptures of people, places, and historical events

Objectives: To review and deepen comprehension

Grade levels: 2 to 6

Materials: None

Group size: Small groups or entire class

Classroom setup: Clear space

Living Map:
Procedure & Dialogue

1. Have the class create a map of a particular county or city. Here the topic will be a map of Washington, D.C.

   'We've been studying Washington, D.C., and today we are going to create a living map of the city right here in front of the class.'

2. Designate north, south, east, and west in your room. Then discuss the location. Get volunteers to come up one by one and create a living sculpture (see "Statues One and Two") of each component of the map.

   'Who can name one important building or monument in Washington, D.C.? Ronnie said the Washington Monument. Ronnie, come up here and take a pose that looks like the Washington Monument. Use your arms, trunks, and legs to create a shape like the Washington Monument. Now Ronnie, put your eyes on a particular spot on the wall or on the ceiling and hold that pose. There's our Washington Monument. Now what monument is right across from the Washington Monument? Right. Peggy, will you take a pose that reminds us of the Lincoln Memorial? Put your eyes on a spot on the wall or ceiling and hold it. Good. There's our Lincoln Memorial.'

3. If you are working with half the class and building a map one student at a time, the students will not be able to hold their poses for the entire time it takes to set up the map. Simply have the students take their pose and then tell them to relax but to stay in their places until the map is completed.

   'Ronnie and Peggy relax your bodies now, but stay in your place. I'll ask you to take your poses again in a minute when the rest of the map is finished . . .'

The Creative Classroom

4. Once all the components are set, ask the students to assume their poses. Tell the students you will move to each location on the map and you will tap them. When they are tapped ask them to say who they are and why they are important to this city, state, or country, or have them give one important fact about this site.

   'Okay, now we have our map of Washington, D.C. At the count of three I want everyone to take their pose and put their eyes on a particular spot and hold that pose. When you do, I am going to move to each location on this map. When I tap you, I want you to tell us who you are and why you are important to our nation's capital. One . . . two . . . three . . . take your pose.'

5. Move quickly around the map and tap each site.

   '(Student) I am the Lincoln Memorial. I am important to Washington, D.C., because I remind people of our great president, Abraham Lincoln, who set all the slaves free . . .'

6. Urge them to keep their poses until the entire map has spoken.

   'Hold your poses till everyone on our map has spoken. Keep your eyes on a particular place and keep them there.'

7. Close the activity. You may want to take a real or imaginary picture of the map to provide one last strong visual image for those who are observing (see "Living Web, Lesson One").

   'Now I have my imaginary camera with me. I'm going to take a picture of our map. So hold your poses, hold your poses—great, I got it! And relax! Good job—let's give them a hand.'

8. Feel free to create a second map with the other half of the class. Try to include other sites.

Living Time Line

Instead of creating a map, create a time line of events. For instance, events leading up to the Revolutionary War, important Civil War battles, important stages in world or art history, or even key moments in a story or book.

The students follow the same basic procedure outlined above. They create poses for a sequence of events that are presented in the proper order. When you tap them, they say the name of their event and a significant fact about the event.

Modifications

1. These activities can also be done as group work. Give each group a topic and let them create the sequence, the poses, and what they are going to say. Give the students time to rehearse, and then let each group present their sculptures to the class. You may want to do a full class map or time line prior to breaking the students into groups so that expectations are clear.

2. You can also extend this activity by adding "Role Play, Lesson Three." Then you can interview the various components of the time line or map. Famous buildings, people, and events can actually speak and talk about themselves.

3. You can also extend the activity by adding "Environment Orchestra." Then sounds can be added to the various locations.

4. In one class we created a map of Washington, D.C., and added a tour bus to the map that moved from one place to another. As it arrived at a site, the tour guide announced the location and then the building came to life and gave a brief report about its history.

5. You may want to repeat the activity for full effectiveness.

6. Paragraphing can also be taught through this game. Give a group of students a paragraph. Have them create a living sculpture of the paragraph that shows where the topic sentence is in relation to the supporting sentences. For instance, if the topic sentence is the first sentence, then all the supporting ideas would be below it. Have the students present the "Living Paragraph" to the class as they read each sentence in the paragraph. The rest of the students should be able to see which sentence is the topic.

Personal Notes & Adaptations

Then What Happened?

Overview: Students create a group story by continually answering the question, "Then what happened?"

Objectives: To reinforce sequence and logic
To increase problem-solving abilities
To create an original story line

Grade level: PreK to 6

Materials: None

Group size: Entire class

Classroom setup: At desks

Procedure & Dialogue

1. Provide students with an interesting opening sentence. Here are several examples: "The zookeeper opened the lion's cage very early this morning," "Norma woke up suddenly in the middle of the night," or "Alan and Connie took a long walk in the woods and found a strange bone on the path." In this lesson the sentence being used is, "The zookeeper opened the lion's cage very early this morning."

2. Ask "why" questions to develop the story line.

   '*Who can tell me why he did that? Then what happened?*'

3. Continue to ask the same questions and let students respond. As they do, a story will develop.

   '*Why did that happen? Then what happened?*'

4. Keep the activity going for as long as responses are interesting and fun.

5. Guide the story toward development and conclusion.

6. Act out the story (see "Acting Out a Story").

Activity Variations

1. Each student can add one sentence to the story. Then students can write or draw the story they created.

2. Bring the story to a point of conflict and then break the students into groups and have them complete the story and act it out.

3. As a culminating activity for any unit, select a theme from the unit as a point of departure for the story.

4. Pair up the students. One can write the story, and the other can illustrate it.

5. Create a "Swip Swap Story." Pair up the students. Each partner should have a different color writing utensil. For instance, one could use a pencil and one a pen. Have the partners complete the story you started through this activity, by adding one sentence (paragraph) to the story and then passing the paper to their partner who adds an equal amount to the story. The pairs keep swapping until the story is complete.

   You can use this same technique with a group of students. Then the group could act out a key scene from the story (see "Acting Out a Story").

6. Use the question, "Then what happened?" to review a science lab the students observed or to review a field trip or other experience the class has shared. Write the key ideas on the board. Then have the students find a way to act out these moments.

Comments

This is a good oral composing and prewriting activity.

This is a good activity for vocabulary development and peer cooperation.

This activity helps students understand the motivation behind an action.

Personal Notes & Adaptations

Pizza/Submarine Sandwich/Picnic

Overview: Students create and use an imaginary object

Objectives: To stimulate the imagination
To recall and recite a sequence
To extend memory skills

Grade level: PreK to 6

Materials: None

Group size: Small group or entire class

Classroom setup: A circle

Procedure & Dialogue

All three of these activities are similar in structure. "Pizza" will be used as the example for the following procedural outline.

1. Preset the class.

   '*Today we are going to pretend and use our imaginations to create a giant pizza on the floor in front of us.*'

2. Relax.

   '*I want you to close your eyes and just sit comfortably.*'

3. Have the class imagine that in the circle in front of them is a giant pizza crust. Tell them they are each going to add one ingredient in order to make one huge pizza for the class.

   '*When I count to three, you'll open your eyes and in front of us, if we use our imaginations, will be a giant pizza crust. Everyone will get to add one ingredient to our pizza. So know what you'd like to add when I call on you. Ready. One . . . two . . . three.*'

4. Explain the rules. Note: As students add ingredients, sooner or later a few strange items get added. Be sure they understand they all have to eat the pizza. This is a rule of the activity.

   '*We'll go around the circle, and each of us will add one ingredient to the pizza. Everyone must eat the pizza once we've completed it.*'

5. Begin to add ingredients. Each student pantomimes placing one item on the pizza and says what it is.

'Anna, you go first. Let's see what she's going to add. It looks like she's pouring something all over the crust. Tell us what it is, Anna. Of course! Tomato sauce!'

6. You may want to introduce the memory component of the game. The students recall and recite all the ingredients the class puts on their pizza (see "Grandmother's Trunk"). If remembering all the items is too difficult, just have the class remember in sets of six.

'Anna, now say this line, "On our pizza we put . . . " and fill in your ingredient. Now, Tommy, you're next. What did he add? Cheese! Right. Tommy, now you repeat the line and fill in Anna's ingredient and then your own. "On our pizza we put tomato sauce and cheese."'

7. Have the class eat the pizza.

'Now everybody get out your pizza slicer and cut a piece of pizza. Hold up your slice. Let's eat it together. Go!'

8. Close the activity.

'Now close your eyes. At the count of three, our pizza will be gone and we'll be done eating. Ready? One . . . two . . . three.'

Alternatives

"Submarine Sandwich" is structured in exactly the same way, except a giant sub roll is used.

"Picnic" is structured the same way, except a giant picnic basket is used.

Activity Variations

1. Alphabetical order can be imposed on the activity, or an adjective can be added to describe each ingredient (see "Grandmother's Trunk").

2. The activity can be modified to be used as a prewriting activity for a creative writing assignment: "For whom are we making this pizza? Why? Where do we have to take it?" and so on.

Personal Notes & Adaptations

5

Activities That Deepen Comprehension & Promote Writing Skills
Visualization

The activities in this section are designed to promote receptive and expressive language skills. They are also designed to help students synthesize information, thereby deepening their comprehension. Many of the creative drama games in this section contain a visualization component either in the preset or as a main part of the activity.

Visualization means picturing images in one's imagination that are oftentimes stimulated by a series of verbal sensory cues. Although games and activities introduced earlier used some visualization, you will find it is used in greater depth in the techniques presented in this chapter.

Recently, visualization has become a very popular tool in a variety of spheres including business, stress management, therapy, and even in the athletic training for the Olympic Games. It is an excellent tool for relaxing, focusing, and picturing oneself capable of achieving one's goals.

Actors have used visualization for years. Through visualization, an actor can "see" a character he or she is being asked to portray or recall a place, a feeling, or an event that may be helpful in creating a role. Playwrights use visualization in order "to hear" the voice and words of characters they are creating.

The activities "Guided Imagery" and "Sound Trip" use visualization in its pure form. The students close their eyes and picture various mental images. Through visualization, students relax and focus. It calms them and helps to build an environment ripe for creativity. It prepares students and helps them understand what is expected of them within the confines of the activity. It increases the students' listening skills in that they must follow instructions, associate ideas, and conceptualize.

Students love to visualize. They look forward to it. Small children (PreK to 1) often have difficulty keeping their eyes closed for an extended period, yet their imaginations are so rich that they can open and close their eyes very quickly and instantly see images in their minds. Other students need to have their eyes closed for longer periods in order for images to appear.

New content material can easily be introduced through some of these activities. There are also a number of review tools. Many can serve as excellent prewriting and composing activities.

Guided Imagery

Overview: Students visualize images in their imagination that are stimulated by verbal cues

Objectives: To strengthen listening skills
To promote concentration

Grade level: PreK to 6

Materials: None

Group size: Entire class

Classroom setup: At desks

Guided imagery is a pure form of visualization. It consists of students closing their eyes and visualizing various images in their imaginations. These images are stimulated by a set of verbal sensory cues provided by the teacher. The following are three samples of guided imagery lessons. They are arranged in order, from simple to more complex. You may use them as is and/or as models for visualizations you create.

After a "Guided Imagery" or "Sound Trip" lesson, students are often very relaxed. Sometimes, they are moved or surprised by all that they have envisioned. If the students are uncomfortable sharing verbally what they saw in their minds, ask them to write or draw the experience. Often, students are so motivated to write, it is difficult to get them to stop.

If some students resist closing their eyes, do not harp at them to do so. This can ruin the relaxed and creative environment you are trying to create for the class as a whole. Also, if some students do not see any images with their eyes closed, tell them not to worry. Gently encourage them to relax, keep their eyes closed, and listen. Eventually images will appear.

Guided Imagery, Lesson 1 (PreK to 6)

This is a short beginning lesson. It can be used to get the students familiar with visualization.

Procedure & Dialogue

1. Preset the class.

'Today we are going to use our imaginations to pretend all sorts of things. But in order for us to do this, we'll have to close our eyes.'

2. Encourage relaxation.

   'First clear your desks of everything. Close your eyes and put your head on your desk.'

3. Initiate color visualization.

   'Now with your eyes closed, I want you to see in your imagination your favorite color.'

4. Check cohesiveness of the class.*

   'When you see this color, I want you to keep your eyes and mouth closed, but raise your hand or finger so I know we are together.'

5. Initiate odor recall.

   'Now a wonderful smell starts to tickle your nose. At first you're not sure what the smell is, but soon it is clear. Identify it. Know what it is.'

6. Check cohesiveness.

   'When you smell this odor, I want you to keep your eyes and mouth closed, but raise your hand or finger so I know we are together.'

7. Initiate sound recall.

   'Now a distant sound is heard. Listen . . . it's getting louder and louder. Identify it. Really hear it booming in your ears.'

8. Check cohesiveness.

   'When you hear this sound, I want you to keep your eyes and mouth closed, but raise your hand or finger so I know we are together.'

9. Initiate taste recall.

   'Now your favorite food appears. It looks delicious. It's just the way you like it, and there is a lot of it!'

---

* Please note: Checking on the cohesiveness of the class can be done after each segment or sporadically throughout the lesson.

10. Check cohesiveness. (Older students may be hesitant to eat the food with their eyes open. If so, let them eat it in their imaginations.)

   'When I count to three, I want you to imagine that your favorite food is in front of you. Then we'll open our eyes and take a bite. One . . . two . . . three.'

11. The class can then share what they ate, smelled, saw, heard, and so on. PreK-1 students can pretend to wash their faces and hands after their imaginary meal (see "Food Pantomime").

   'Who will tell me what they ate? What sounds did you hear? Oh, no! Our faces and hands are a mess from all we ate. We'd better wash up.'

12. Pass around an imaginary garbage can in which they can put their crumbs and napkins.

   'Now put your napkins in my trash can and brush the crumbs off the tops of your desks.'

13. Close the activity.

   'Now close your eyes one more time, and when I count to three, we will no longer be pretending, our food will be gone, and our imaginary trip over. We will be back in our classroom. One . . . two . . . three.'

Comments

As interest and attention spans increase, you can add more involved sensory segments. Examples may be an object appearing in their minds, something rubbing against their legs, or textured objects that they explore in their imagination.

Expect young children to call out what they are seeing, smelling, and hearing. This just means they are excited by what they are experiencing. Be gentle and encourage them to listen once again.

Personal Notes & Adaptations

Guided Imagery, Lesson 2 (Grades 1 to 6)

This lesson motivates students to create their own ending to a story. It also provides them with ideas to share and develop after the visualization.

Procedure & Dialogue

1. Preset the class.

   'Today we are going on an imaginary adventure in our minds. Clear your desks and close your eyes so I know you are ready to go.'

2. Encourage relaxation.

   'Sit comfortably and try to stay focused on the sound of my voice.'

3. Establish place.

   'Picture in your imagination your favorite place—a place that makes you happy to think about. It may be someplace you've really been or an imaginary place.'

4. Check cohesiveness of the class.

   'If you can see this place in your mind, raise your hand so I know we are together.'

5. Develop sensory awareness.

   'What colors do you see in your favorite place? What smells do you smell? Listen to the sounds in this wonderful place. Now pick up something in your imaginary place; explore it with your hands; note its color, shape, texture, and smell. (Pause between questions to give students a chance to visualize.)'

6. Check class cohesiveness.

   When you have found this object, I want you to keep your eyes and mouth closed, but raise your hand so I know we are together.

7. Continue to develop sensory awareness.

   'Now find your favorite food and smell it and taste it. Enjoy the wonderful taste of that food.'

The Creative Classroom

8. Develop a story.

'Suddenly in your food you find a note—a message. The message tells you about something you must do immediately. Stop eating and hurry and do whatever the note says. When you are done, you can come back to your favorite place. I will count to ten, and when I finish counting you will need to have completed your task. One . . . two . . . three . . ., ten. Your task needs to be completed now, so relax.'

9. Close the activity.

'Take a minute now to take one last look at your favorite place. See it clearly and choose one thing you'd like to bring back from this place to share with the class. At the count of five, you will come back from your special place with whatever you want to share, and you will find yourself back at your desk. Your journey back can be by boat, hot air balloon, jet, fancy car, or on a bicycle—any way you choose. Find your transportation back to school and be on your way. One . . . two . . . three . . . four . . . five . . .'

10. Have the students share what they brought back and what their messages told them to do.

11. After the students share aspects of their adventure, they can act out scenes or draw or write their stories.

Personal Notes & Adaptation

Guided Imagery, Lesson 3
(Grades 1 to 6)

This lesson provides students with a story starter and then allows for student creativity. This type of visualization works well as a literature extension lesson.

Procedure & Dialogue

1. Preset the class.

   '*Please clear your desks of everything. Today we are going on another adventure in our minds. We are going to imagine that we are all detectives. We are going to solve a mystery. So close your eyes, close your eyes . . .* '

2. Encourage relaxation.

   '*Sit comfortably and relax. You can put your heads on your desk if you want to. Try to listen carefully to everything I say.*'

3. Establish place and sense awareness.

   '*Imagine a new place, a new city, somewhere you've never been. It is a very strange and interesting place—filled with new people and things you've never seen before. Look all around this place. See all the colors. Note the smells, sounds . . .* '

4. Check class cohesiveness.

   '*If you are in this new place, raise your hand so I know we are together.*'

5. Set the task or purpose.

   '*You are here for a reason. You are a great detective and have been asked by the leader of this city to come here to help him. The rare, beautiful Clock of the World has lost its golden hand and without it, time is standing still. Take a moment to think—if time is standing still what is or isn't happening in the world? What would happen if time stood still forever?*

   You have been sent here to solve the mystery and find the missing hand.'

6. Develop and define a story. (As students become familiar with visualization, this part can get less and less structured.)

'Who do you need to see? Are there any likely suspects? Who might want time to stand still? Did the hand simply disappear? If so, how did that happen, and where is it? Take a minute to gather the information you need and see the people you think will help you. (Pause for a minute.) Finish gathering your information and decide where you will find the golden hand.'

7. Set limits so success can be achieved. (Freedom is given to imagine, but limits help the group stay together.)

   'You now have to the count of 30 to locate the golden hand. One . . . two . . . three . . . , thirty.'

8. Check for class cohesiveness.

   'Keep your eyes closed, but raise your hand if you found the golden hand. For those who did not, look down in front of your right foot, and there you will see a golden box covered in jewels. Open it and find the beautiful lost golden hand. How did it get there?'

9. Resolve the story.

   'Now replace the hand of the clock, and hear the city cheer in your honor. Then hear the clock ticking and know that time is again on the move. As the bells of the clock chime, once again hear the crowd cheer.'

10. Close the activity.

    'Now take off your detective clothes, and put on your school clothes. Put on a set of wings and fly back to school so that you can share your story. At the count of three, we will be back at our desks. One . . . two . . . three . . . '

11. Have the students share their story orally and/or in written form.

Activity Variations

1. Use this same detective character in other visualizations to extend a story the students have read. For instance, after reading the book *Jumanji, A Jungle Adventure Game* by Chris Van Allsburg, have the detective secretly investigate the inventor of the game. The detective received a tip that the inventor has created a new game. What is it? What is it called? What will it do? Why does the inventor create these games?

2. After the students have studied a particular country or time period, take them on a journey in their minds to that place or time.

   a. Have the students visualize themselves as colonists coming to America. Have them feel the rocking boat and feel the hunger the colonists felt.

   b. Have the students imagine themselves on the Underground Railroad being led by Harriet Tubman. What did they see, hear, experience? Have them bring an object back to share with the class.

   Using visualization in relation to a historical time period is very effective. It deepens students' comprehension of history and their awareness of the feelings and experiences of others.

3. Create a visualization around a concept in science. Have the students visualize themselves as a caterpillar becoming a butterfly or as a blood cell in the human body.

Activity Extensions

1. Have the students act out, write, or draw any or all parts of their visualizations (see "Acting Out a Story").

Personal Notes & Adaptations

ound Trip

Overview: Students visualize a story line in their imaginations; music is used as the stimulus for the visualizations

Objectives: To stimulate the imagination
To compose an original story

Grade level: PreK to 6

Materials: Instrumental music (preferably classical, soundtracks, or New Age) or sound effects records. Opera can also be used, if the selection is sung in a language that the students do not understand.

Group size: Entire class

Classroom setup: At desks

Procedure & Dialogue

1. Preset the class.

   'Are you ready to go on another voyage in our minds? Good. Then clear your desks.'

2. Encourage relaxation.

   'I want you to close your eyes and just sit comfortably and listen carefully.'

3. Explain that you are going to play some music and that you want the music to take them on an imaginary journey.

   'I'm going to play some music, and I want you to listen to the music and let it take you to an imaginary place and on an imaginary adventure.'

4. Initiate the visualization: Play the music.

   'Just listen to the music. Keep your eyes closed. What does the music remind you of? Where does it take you? What do you see? Don't tell me, just listen.'

5. Check cohesiveness of the class.

   'Raise your hand or finger if you can see an imaginary place.'

6. Build a story.

   'Now see what else the music brings to mind. See if there's some adventure, story, or scene this music is telling you.'

7. Check cohesiveness of the class.

   '*Keep your eyes closed, but raise your hand if you have a story unfolding in your imagination.*'

8. Close the activity. This needs to be timed with the end of the musical selection.

   '*Finish your story now. The music is ending. When I count to three, you will open your eyes, be here in the classroom, and, if you want to, you can share your story with the other students. One . . . two . . . three.*'

9. Share stories or aspects of the stories.

10. Students can then write, act, or draw some or all of their adventures (see "Acting Out a Story").

Alternate Ending

Play more than one selection of music. Vary the type of music you play. The students can then discuss and compare the music and the different images it brought forth.

Activity Variations

1. Use "Sound Trip" as a prewriting activity for an original play. Have the students act out the play with the music playing in the background.

2. Tell the students to imagine they are in a particular location before playing the selection. It can also be a location the class is presently studying.

3. Select music in connection with a particular time period or culture being studied.

Comments

Keep the musical selections short for grades PreK to 2. These students may need to open and close their eyes continually, but don't focus upon that. Just gently remind them to close their eyes.

Be sure to listen to the musical selection before you play it for the class. See if it brings images to mind for you. Usually if it works for you, it will work for your students.

Personal Notes & Adaptation

Texture Walk/Mobile Words

Overview: Students move in a number of different ways and through a variety of imaginary textures

Objectives: To develop vocabulary
To stimulate the imagination

Grade level: 1 to 6

Materials: None

Group size: Small groups or entire class

Classroom setup: A clear open space: gym, cafeteria, or outdoors

Texture Walk:
Procedure & Dialogue

1. Preset the class.

   'Today we are going to use our imaginations and go for a walk in a number of different places. I'll be asking you to walk around the room and to stop when I say "Stop!" Then I'll ask you to close your eyes and tell you where we are going to be in our imaginations.'

2. Have the students walk around the room.

   'Are you ready? So let's walk around the room. No talking please.'

3. Once a quiet rhythm is established, ask them to stop, close their eyes and imagine that they are walking through various textures, *e.g.,* walking on hot sand, wading in the water; struggling through snow drifts; skating on ice; fighting a strong wind; walking through peanut butter, ice cream, or hot fudge; and so on.

   'Stop! Close your eyes. I want you to imagine that you are no longer in this classroom. Instead I want you to imagine that you are at the beach walking on very hot sand. Open your eyes and start walking.'

4. Encourage the students to really feel the texture. If it feels good, urge them to enjoy it. If it feels bad, urge them to fight their way through it.

   'The sand is so hot it's burning your feet. You have no shoes on, and the sand is very hot. Keep walking. Now finally you get to the water and you feel much better. Walk

*and wade in cool water. Really enjoy the feeling. Stop!
Close your eyes! Now, I want you to imagine you are walking in snow that is up to your knees. Open your eyes and
start walking. It is very hard to walk. Really push against the
snow; push harder . . . '*

5. Close the activity.

   *'Stop! Now close your eyes and at the count of three we'll
   open our eyes and be back here in the classroom. One . . .
   two . . . three.'*

6. Discuss the various sensations.

   *'Did you enjoy that activity? How did it feel when you
   were walking on the hot sand? Which texture did you like
   the best? Which one really bothered you? (And so on.)'*

Mobile Words:
Procedure & Dialogue

"Mobile Words" begins the same way. Follow steps 1 and 2 of
"Texture Walk."

3. Instead of textures, have students respond to different verbs
   that involve movement and change their movements to fit
   the verbs. Here is a list of possible verb choices: stretch,
   bend, turn, wiggle, writhe, sway, expand, contract, curl,
   uncurl, sink, sag, slouch, droop, squirm, creep, collapse,
   flip, leap, whirl, stroll, strut, meander, limp, hop, hobble,
   scramble, roll, scurry, amble, dodge . . .

   *'Begin stretching across the room. Stretch your legs, arms,
   fingers, necks! Keep moving and really stretch. Stop! Now I
   want you to droop around the room. Let your head, neck,
   arms, legs—everything—let it droop! Keep moving and
   drooping. Let me see your eyes and mouth droop! Stop!
   Now . . . '*

4. You can lead the activity and show the students the meaning of the verbs or use the game as an assessment tool for
   verbs previously introduced. Students will deepen their
   understanding of these verbs by doing the exercise.

5. You need not use the visualization component as in
   "Texture Walk." The students do not need to close their
   eyes and imagine themselves in other locations for this
   activity.

6. Close the activity.

Activity Variations

1. For PreK to 1, children can become animals or community helpers as they walk.

2. This activity can be a motivation for the development of a class thesaurus or book of synonyms or antonyms.

3. Texture rubbings can be used as a follow up to "Texture Walks."

4. The game can also be modified to teach adverbs.

Comments

This is a great review exercise for new vocabulary words in that it provides full sensory experience with new words and environments.

Be sure to provide concrete stimulus and/or a model for PreK to 1 students to imitate before doing the activity.

Personal Notes & Adaptations

6

Activities That Promote Language & Thinking Skills
Role Play

Role play is the act of pretending to be someone or something you're not. This technique is an excellent way to elevate attention and focus energy in the classroom. Role play also motivates students to listen, think, and speak.

Over the years I've done role plays with students in which we've been the sun, the Earth, the moon, and the stars for a unit on solar energy. I've played a firefighter, named Officer Clark, who told a story about fire safety in the home. And teachers I've worked with have conducted lessons as construction workers, the Governor of Alabama during the Reconstruction Period, and a bear getting ready for hibernation.

A third-grade teacher I was working with in Minneapolis came to school in the dead of winter (–20 F) in a thin blue cotton jumpsuit and jeweled open-toed sandals. She said to me, "Can you guess who I am today?" I hadn't a clue. She proudly stated, "I'm the Caribbean Ocean for our lesson today. How do you like it?" I was speechless.

While doing a residency at an elementary school in Alaska, I conducted an evening staff development session with teachers. The workshop ended at 9:00 P.M. By 9:00 A.M., the speech pathologist was dancing down the hallway in a full-length Wizard costume (which she made overnight), announcing that she was the famous and daring "Word Wizard"! Once again, I was amazed.

Anything is possible with role play. It allows you to bring countless guests into your classroom and to change the classroom environment to new locations; and all you need are a few props and/or costume pieces and your imagination.

Preparing to Take on a Role

The more you or your students look and/or sound like someone else, the more exciting the role play. Wearing a hat, a shawl, a scarf, or an apron really helps to change your appearance. Collect interesting hats, jackets, skirts, fabric, tinsel, and the like, and keep them in a big box in your room. Have the students bring in items, too.

Don't worry if you are not an actor. Try changing your voice, pitch, pace, or accent. Try changing your facial expression, walk or manner—anything that makes you sound or look different.

Here are some simple steps to follow as you create a role:

1. For young children (PreK – Grade 1) reality and fantasy can be confusing. Prepare the children by explaining that you are going to pretend to be someone else. Then show them the costume piece or prop you will use to become the character. Tell them the name of the person you are about to become: "When I put on this firefighter's cap, I will pretend to be Officer Clark. Who am I really? That's right. I'm Mrs. Kelner, but when I put on this hat I will be Firefighter Clark. Are you ready to meet her?"

2. For older students, when first using role play, explain who you are going to become but do not show them the costume piece or prop. Let it be a surprise.

3. Turn your back to the class and put on your costume. If possible, assume the posture and face of the character as well.

4. When you turn around and face the class, you are the character. If possible, speak in the character's voice and manner. If in the middle of the role play you need to address an issue as the teacher (because of a behavior problem or a knock at the classroom door, for example), take off one piece of your costume, be yourself, and deal with the problem. Then put the costume piece back on and resume the character.

5. When you've completed the role play, turn your back to the class again, and take off your costume. Turn around, face the class and be yourself again.

   For younger children (PreK – Grade 1) ask the children, "Who am I really? And who did I pretend to be?" This helps to confirm in their minds, that you have returned to reality.

6. If you use role play often, feel free to modify the way in which you and your students move from reality to fantasy and back to reality. You may use a sound effect, a word, a chant, or simply ask them to close their eyes. But the important point is that the activity should have a clear beginning, middle, and end.

7. When you first use role play in your classroom, keep it short, especially for younger children. The more you do role plays, the longer they can become.

8. If several students are taking on roles, ask them to follow a similar procedure as outlined in steps 1–6 above. Be sure the class knows who they are becoming so expectations are clear.

9. In group role plays, ask that every group member speak at least one sentence in the presentation. This stops one or two students from taking over.

10. If the entire class takes on a role then add these steps (see "Role Play, Lesson Two"):

    a. Have the students clear the tops of their desks or their hands of anything that is not appropriate for the fictional situation they are about to create.

    b. Explain to the students the purpose and goal(s) of the role play.

    c. In the role plays you do with the entire class, the teacher should take on a role of leadership or authority to help direct and focus the role play.

    d. Have the students enter the fictional world of the role play together. Have everyone put on one last costume piece at the same time, and let that signal that the role play has begun; or have all the students put on their name tags with their fictional characters' names at the same time, and let that be a signal that the role play has started.

e. Set up a device that ends the role play before you even begin. For instance, you might say, "When I take off my hat (name tag, scarf, or whatever) that means the role play is over, and it's time for us to be ourselves again," or "When I say 'Thank you very much for coming to the meeting today' that means the role play is over, and we are ourselves again."

f. Often older students need only a few minutes to plan or prepare their role plays. However, sometimes you may want to assign roles the day before so that students can read appropriate material, gather costumes, and prepare the role. This is particularly true when the role play focuses on historical figures or events or for book reports.

Following these simple steps will help keep reality and fantasy clear and help the students know what is expected of them as they take on roles.

Ways to Use Role Play

Role play can be used across the curriculum. I've used role play with all grade levels of students, PreK to grade 12. They can be short (two to three minutes), or long (30 to 40 minutes), or last over the course of several days. The role play can involve just the teacher or the entire class. Here are a few suggestions on how to use role play in your classroom:

- Tell the students a story in character. Then let students retell the story in character (see "Role Play, Lesson One").

- Involve the entire class in a role play in which they bring to life the issues raised in a story or in a moment in history. For example, after the students have read *The Great Kapok Tree* by Lynne Cherry, have the students role play a conference of the International Woodcutters Association. Some students can play a toucan, a jaguar, an emerald tree boa, a Brazilian tree frog, a tree porcupine, and a kapok tree who have come to the conference to persuade the woodcutters to stop cutting down the rain forest. The remaining students are woodcutters at the conference. After hearing the animals' stories, the Association must make a decision as to what to do regarding the rain forest (see "Role Play, Lesson Two").

- Ask a group of students to become a numerator, a denominator, a fraction line, a proper fraction, an improper fraction, and an equivalent fraction. Have them speak in the first person and show and tell what they are and their relationship to the other things in the group.

- Recreate the life cycle of a plant, a caterpillar, or a moth by having the students become the roots, a cocoon, or the like. Recreate the water cycle. Any process or cycle lends itself beautifully to role play.

- Interview an author of a book. Why did he or she write the book? What does he or she hope you will remember about the book?

- Use role play as an alternative to book reports. Have the students present their reports as the main character in the book or as an important object in the story. The students may even want to tell the story from the perspective of a minor character or an animal in the story. Try to avoid a linear retelling of the story. Provide questions to the students that promote critical thinking and assess comprehension such as: What were the two most significant things that happened to you in this story? What secret dream did you have? Did you achieve it? If not, why not? What moments made you feel proud? embarrassed?

- Create a continuous character who returns often to the class to teach a particular subject. For instance, "Chef Gumbo" may be a character who facilitates all your cooking lessons, or "The Magic Queen of Letters" may be a character who conducts lessons on consonant sounds or spelling. "Professor Schnoze" may be a scientist who leads the students through various scientific experiments.

  Please note: Nose glasses (glasses with eyebrows, nose and mustache attached) are a fun and simple way for you to turn into someone else. You can usually find them at a toy or party store. Students love them!

- Create a character who knows less than the students. This type of character motivates the students to help and promotes language, thinking skills, and comprehension (see "Role Play, Lesson One").

These are just a few examples of how you can use role play in your classroom. The uses of this technique are limited only by your imagination.

On the following pages, you will find several activities that include some form of role play.

In Lessons One, Two, and Three of "Role Play" the technique is presented in its purest form. I've included both primary and intermediate level lessons. In Lesson One, the teacher presents a lesson as a character. Lesson Two utilizes the entire class. Lesson Three involves random students. Use these lessons as models for creating your own role plays.

Imaginary Mask

Overview: Students put on an imaginary mask that reflects the face or feelings of someone else

Objective: To explore feelings

Grade level: PreK to 3

Materials: None

Group size: Entire class or small group

Classroom setup: No particular setup necessary

Procedure & Dialogue

1. Ask the students to reach behind their ears and find masks. Tell them to shake out the masks and hold them in front of them.

   'Reach behind your ear and find a mask. Shake it out and spread it on your open hand in front of you.'

2. Then explain to the students what kind of mask you want them to put on, *i.e.*, Baby Bear in Goldilocks after his chair was smashed, a lost library book, or a child no one will play with.

   'This is the mask of Little Red Riding Hood when she discovers the wolf in Granny's clothes. Now, at the count of three, I want you to put on the mask and let me see how she felt. One . . . two . . . three.'

3. You can comment upon the feelings you observe or interview the characters created by the masks either as a group or individually. You can even use the imaginary microphone for the interviews (see "Guidelines for Success").

   'Oh my, you look so frightened! (Or) How are you feeling Little Red Riding Hood? Who do you see?'

Modifications

Have half of the class put on the masks and the other half describe what they see and then reverse the activity.

Comments

Be sure you do the activity right along with the students when you first introduce it. That will help the students understand what is expected of them.

This is a great way to introduce role play to students.

This is a terrific activity for exploring differing viewpoints and feelings.

Personal Notes & Adaptations

Statues One & Statues Two

Overview: Students become statues of various characters and/or emotions

Objectives: To deepen comprehension
To identify and explore emotions
To increase concentration

Grade level: K to 6

Materials: None

Group size: Small group or entire class

Classroom setup: A circle or a clear space

Statues One:
Procedure & Dialogue

1. Discuss the properties of a statue with the class.

   'What is a statue? What are statues made of?'

2. Preset the class.

   'Now I want all of you to pretend to become a statue.'

3. Introduce the concepts of "freeze" and "melt." Students will become statues on "freeze" and resume normal activity on "melt." Experiment with this several times. Tell them to focus their eyes on a particular spot on the wall or ceiling. This will help them stay frozen.

   'When I say the word, "Freeze!" I want you to imagine you are a statue and that you cannot move at all. When I say, "Melt!" you can relax and be yourselves again. Let's try it. "Freeze!" Put your eyes on a particular spot on the wall and keep them there. It might be a crack in the wall or the light switch, but just keep staring right at that dot; it will help you stay still. Keep staring at it. Really freeze now! Don't move an inch! Now, "Melt!" Good. Let's try it again.'

4. Select five students. Ask them to stand, and select an emotion they would like to portray.

   Please note: For grades K and 1, begin by choosing one emotion for all five students to portray.

5. Say "Freeze," and have them become statues of those emotions.

6. The class observes the statues and guesses what feeling is being portrayed.

7. Then have the statues melt.

8. Discuss the reasons people have for feeling these various emotions.

   'What kinds of things make us feel scared? What makes us feel mad?'

9. Close the activity.

   'You did a great job pretending we were statues today. Now close your eyes. At the count of three, we'll be done pretending we are statues and we will be ourselves again. 1 . . . 2 . . . 3.'

Activity Variations

1. The statues can come to life one by one and speak.

2. The statues can also be characters from a story the students have read. Have the rest of the class guess what character is being portrayed.

3. Students can imagine that they are a statue or mannequin in an unfamiliar setting. What do they see, hear, and feel?

4. Students can imagine that they are a doll or toy that comes alive at night.

5. Have the students imagine that a statue of a famous person of another time period comes to life in today's world. Let the character talk to the students. This is a great alternative to a written report.

Comments

See "Living Map/Living Time Line," "Bits 'n Pieces," and "Becoming Objects" as extensions of this activity.

Statues Two, Grades 2–6: Procedure & Dialogue

1. Follow steps 1 through 3 of "Statues One."

2. Break the students into groups (four to six students per group).

3. Give each group an index card. On the card should be written a significant event from a story the students have read or from a period in history they are studying. Here the topic is the Civil War for students in grade 5.

The group must create a sculpture that reflects the event stated on the card.

'Each group take one of these cards. On the card you will find written an important Civil War event. I want you to create a group sculpture that shows us something about this event and the feelings involved in that moment in time.'

4. Do one sculpture in front of the class so they understand what is being asked of them.

'For instance, let's say we were going to do a sculpture of the Treaty of Appomatox. What or who would we need?

Right! Ulysses S. Grant and Robert E. Lee. James, would you be General Grant; and Wayne, will you be Robert E. Lee?

Where would they be?

At a table? Phillip, will you be our table? We'll put this piece of paper on it as the Treaty. How are these men feeling?

Yes, General Lee is very discouraged, and General Grant is very proud. How can we show that?

Good! We could have General Lee seated on a chair and General Grant standing with his foot on a chair.

Now, who else might have been there or was there perhaps in spirit?

Yes, we could have some freed slaves and some plantation owners. Let's get the five of you to be our freed slaves. How are they feeling? Right, joyous. How can we show that with our bodies?

What about the plantation owners—how are they feeling? Very angry—yes. How can we show that?'

5. Say "Freeze!" and have them take their poses.

'Now when I say "Freeze!" I want you to take your poses and show us the sculpture entitled "The Treaty of Appomatox." One . . . two . . . three . . . Freeze!'

6. Tap the shoulders of each person in the statue, and ask them to say who they are and how they are feeling at this moment in time and why.

*'This sculpture is entitled "The Treaty of Appomatox."
When I tap you on the shoulder, tell me who you are and
what you are feeling at this moment.'*

7. Have the students relax and applaud them.

    *'Good job. Let's see our sculpture one last time. Now
    "Melt!" and relax. Let's give them a hand.'*

8. Have students create their own sculpture in groups and
   repeat this process. Feel free to take a real or imaginary
   picture of the statues.

Comments

Students really enjoy this activity. It challenges students to think
and synthesize the information they have learned. The activity
can be very moving for you and for your students.

Personal Notes & Adaptations

Plants on the Grow

Overview: An activity in which the growing process for plants is acted out

Objectives: To reinforce knowledge about the growing process

Grade level: PreK to 1

Materials: A real plant with roots exposed and/or a picture of a plant that includes the roots

Group size: Small group or entire class

Classroom setup: A clear space that allows students to move

Procedure & Dialogue

1. Discuss with the students what a plant needs to grow. Be sure to include the seed, soil, water, sunshine, and air. Also discuss the parts of a plant. Explain to them that the deeper the roots go into the ground, the taller the plant grows above the ground. Use the song and gestures below to help illustrate this concept.

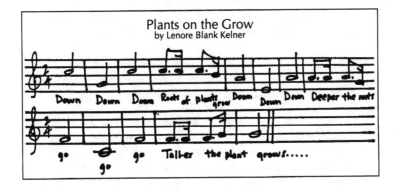

Plants on the Grow
by Lenore Blank Kelner

Variation One: The students use one hand flat out as the ground level and the other hand as the roots going down below the ground's surface. Each time the word "down" or "go" is said, the children's hands go lower and lower below the surface of the ground:

Down
  Down
    Down
      Roots of plants grow
Down
  Down
    Down
Deeper the roots
Go
  Go
    Go
Taller the tree (plant)
  Grows UP! (Shout)

Then when the plant grows, the moving hand curves upward through the ground level and moves upward through the air.

Variation Two: Have the students imagine that their toes are the roots. Have them curl up in a ball and wiggle their toes for each "down" and "go." Then as the plant grows, have them slowly stand and stretch tall.

2. Preset the class.

   '*Now we're going to use our imaginations and become little seeds ourselves and act out the story of how plants grow. So find a space on the floor and sit down.*'

3. Then have the students transform themselves into seeds. They can curl up into a tiny ball. You can then plant them. You can then create sounds for rain, sun, and air.

   '*I want all of you to curl up and become little tiny seeds. Be sure you know what kind of seed you are. I'm going to plant all of these lovely seeds. I'm going to plant this little seed* (touch student's head) *and this one. . . , and this one. . . . Now these beautiful seeds need rain* (sound) *and air* (sound). . .'

4. Encourage the seeds and roots to grow by singing the song "Plants on the Grow." Do this several times until the plants have grown nice and tall.

   '*Now my seeds are starting to grow. I see they're sprouting. If the plant is growing up that means the roots are going down, down into the ground. I'll sing my song again so the roots can grow down deep into the ground and the plants can go up!* (Sing) *Down, down, down roots of plants. . .*'

5. Once grown, interview the plants to find out what type of plant has blossomed. Use the imaginary microphone (see "Guidelines for Success," and "Role Play, Lesson Three/Character Interviews").

   '*Now they are as tall as they can be. Let's see what kinds of plants I have here. I'll just take out my microphone. What type of plant are you? and you?*'

6. Close the activity. Pick each fruit, vegetable, and flower and, as you do, have students return to their seats.

   '*I think I'll pick all my fruits, and when I do, I want you to go back to your seats and be yourselves again. Now, I'll pick all my vegetables, and when I do I want you to go back to your seats. Now I'll pick all my flowers . . .*'

Activity Variations

1. Modify the activity for the fall and the harvest.

2. Conduct the lesson by taking on the character of a farmer (see the introduction to this chapter).

3. This activity can be done with half the class at a time, so that half the class can be seeds and the other half the rain, sun, air, and harvesters. Use the "Motion Sound" activity for students to create motions and sounds for the rain, sun, air, and so on.

Comments

This is an excellent spring and fall activity.

Personal Notes & Adaptations

Role Play, Lesson 1/ ■ A Character in Need

Overview: Teacher transforms into a character who needs help from the students

Objectives: To assess the students' comprehension
To promote language and thinking skills

Grade level: Structure is appropriate for PreK to 3. This lesson is designed for PreK to 1.

Materials: A headband with long braids attached

Group size: Entire class or small group

Classroom setup: A clear space in the front of the room; children can be in a circle, at desks, or on the floor

Procedure & Dialogue

1. Preset the class by explaining who you are going to be and what you want them to do. Be sure to show them the costume before you put it on.

   '*Today we are going to have a visitor. I've asked a little girl named Annie, who's five years old, to come to our class today. You see, Annie hasn't been taking good care of her teeth at all, and I thought since we've been studying about our teeth and good food that you would help Annie. Will you help her? Good. Well, let me show you Annie* (take out the headband).

   This is Annie and when I put on this headband, I'm going to use my imagination and pretend to be Annie. Are you ready for me to put on the headband and pretend to be Annie?'

2. Prepare the students by taking them from reality to fantasy.

   '*Who am I really? That's right, Mrs. Kelner. But when I put on this headband who am I going to pretend to be? Right, Annie. Let's meet her.*'

3. Turn your back and put on the costume.

   '*Oh . . . Annie . . . Annie . . . The children are waiting to meet you.*'

4. Turn around and face the class and speak as the character.

   '*Hi! Hi everyone! My name is Annie and I'm five years old and you know what? I love cookies and cakes and pies!*

You know what I had for breakfast? I had five cookies, a piece of cake, and a glass of soda pop. And you know what I had for dinner last night? Five candy bars, two pieces of pie, some ice cream, and some more soda pop! I think I'll have ten cookies and two candy bars for lunch! That's all I eat—just ice cream and candy, and cookies, and cake, and pies, and I never drink that white stuff you drink—what do you call it? Right . . . milk—I never drink that, and I never brush my teeth, and I never ever ever have gone to the dentist—not ever! (Grab your face in pain) Oww! Oww! Oooohhh! Ohh . . . I smiled too big, and sometimes when I smile real big like that my teeth hurt a real lot, and—Owww Oww Oww (grab face in pain)—and some of my teeth are turning colors. Why do you think that is happening?'

5. Ask questions that help the students identify and solve the character's problem. Repeat appropriate answers for everyone to hear.

   'Why do you think my teeth hurt so much? Owww—Ohh (grab face in pain) Ingres, why do my teeth hurt?

   Because I'm eating too much junk. Well, what's junk?

   Candy and cookies? Why is that junk, Carl? It tastes good!

   Eww . . . they're not good for my teeth? What is good for my teeth? Oww (grab face in pain) . . .

   Milk? Is that stuff good? Oh, I never had any.

   What else should I eat? Apples? Are apples good? Oh, I never had any—what else?'

6. Ask as many questions as the students' attention spans will allow to stimulate language and thinking skills.

   'Besides eating different foods—what else can I do to make my teeth better?'

7. Summarize their answers.

   'You mean if I eat good foods like broccoli and carrots and chicken and apples and cereal and stuff and drink lots of milk my teeth won't hurt?

   And if I eat that stuff I won't get a lot of what was that big word?

   Right, cavities. And I need to go to the dentist and brush my teeth. And if I do all that, my teeth will get better. Do you really think so?

   Well, okay, I'll try. Thanks for being such good friends. I'm glad I came here to talk to you.

   Good-bye . . . bye.'

8. Turn your back to the class, and remove the costume.

9. Turn around and face the class, and return the class to reality.

   'Good-bye Annie. Who am I really? Right, Mrs. Kelner. And who did I pretend to be? Right, Annie. You did a great job helping her. Give yourselves a hand.'

10. Recall and retell the experience.

    'What was wrong with Annie? What did you tell her to eat? What else did you tell her to do?'

Optional

11. Have the students take on the role of Annie and repeat the lesson. Remember boys can be girls and girls can be boys when you are using your imagination.

    If you do this, be prepared for anything. The students may completely change the role play. One student may make Annie a perfect child who brushes her teeth ten times a day. Another student may create an Annie who refuses to change. Try to go with the flow and enjoy the students' creativity.

    'Who would like to come up, put on the headband, pretend to be Annie again, and tell us your story? Philip, will you be Annie? Great.'

12. Follow the same reality and fantasy steps.

    'Who is this really? Right, Philip, but when he puts on this headband who will he pretend to be? Right, Annie.'

13. Have the student turn his or her back and become the character.

    'Oh Annie, come and talk to the children, will you? Oh, here she is . . . Hi Annie! Let's say "Hi" to Annie.'

14. Ask questions of the students to promote language. Kindergarten and first-grade students may have questions they want to ask Annie.

    'How are your teeth Annie? Are you taking better care of them? You are? What are you doing?

    Oh, you are eating lots of fruits and vegetables and you brush after every meal. That's great. And you only eat one cookie a day. That's wonderful.

    Does anyone have a question they'd like to ask Annie?'

15. Ask a question that promotes some independent thinking.

   '*Before you go, Annie, what do you want the children to remember about taking care of their teeth?*

   Be sure to brush! Well, thanks Annie – take care of your-self. Good-bye.'

16. Have the student turn his or her back, take off the costume, and then face the class. This returns the class to reality. Applaud each student.

   '*Let's see who this is. Who is it really?*

   Right, Philip.

   Let's give Philip a hand. Who would like to be Annie next?'

17. Usually three or four students can become the character, and then it's time to close the lesson.

   '*That's all the time we have today. You've done a great job. Give yourselves another big hand. I'm going to put Annie away now, and maybe tomorrow she'll visit us again.*'

Activity Variations

1. Bring Annie back for a second visit and let three or four more students tell her story.

2. Bring Annie back for another visit, have her bring an imaginary (or real) shopping bag, and have the students fill her bag with imaginary foods that are good for her teeth. Let the students find the foods behind an imaginary refrigerator door (see "Imaginary Door").

3. Have the students write Annie an imaginary letter (see "Imaginary Letter"). The students can generate questions for Annie and she can respond.

4. Leave Annie's headband out in the class for students to put on and use.

Modifications

Use the structure of this role play, "A Character in Need," for any subject under study. Students love to help anyone who knows less than they do (see "Shape Game"). For example, you could create a character who does not understand certain math concepts or can't spell.

I've also seen this structure used to sensitize students to the world around them. For instance, I've seen teachers portray a homeless person, a person who is mentally challenged, and a person who cannot speak English very well. This type of role play helps the students understand the concerns and feelings of others.

Comments

Sometimes students say they want to become Annie, put on the headband, and then have nothing to say. If a student wants to sit down, allow them to, and give them applause for coming up. If a student does not want to sit down, but has little to say, ask simple questions he or she can answer with a "yes" or a "no" or a nod of the head. This helps the student feel safe. Follow the same procedure as outlined above, and give them a round of applause at the conclusion.

You may want to read "Role Play, Lessons Two and Three," "Acting Out a Story," "Continuing a Story," "Point of View Switch," and "Object Transformation Two and Three" before doing this activity. It will give you more ideas for using role play and dramatization with students.

Personal Notes & Adaptations

Role Play, Lesson 2/ Full Class Role Play

Overview: Through role play, students explore and expand on a theme or an issue raised in literature and/or history.

Objectives: To promote critical thinking and language
To assess comprehension

Grade level: 2 to 6

Materials: Vary

Group size: Entire class

Classroom setup: A clear space in front of the room with chairs for the main characters; other students can be at desks or in a semi-circle around the chairs.

Procedure & Dialogue

1. Have the class read a story that raises a moral issue, has an unclear resolution, or leaves the reader wondering what will happen next to the characters. Here the fable "The Boy Who Cried Wolf" is used.

2. Create a structure in which the entire class will be involved in bringing the unresolved issue of the story to life. In the first role plays you do with the entire class, create a lead character for the teacher so that you remain in charge of the action. This helps direct the activity and keeps the students focused and on-task.

   '*We all just read Aesop's fable, "The Boy Who Cried Wolf." What do you think happened to the boy after the wolf attacked the citizens' sheep? What do you think the citizens said or did?* (Get some responses) *Well, let's find out. Today we are going to use our imagination, pretend to be the characters in this story, and find out what happened next. We are going to create a town meeting. It is one day after the sheep have been attacked. I will be the mayor of the town.*'

3. Have the students add details that may be missing from the original text.

   '*What name should we give this town? Remember, we can't use anything we've heard on television or in the movies. What name should we give the mayor? Let's get a few names and vote on one . . .*

   So, I am the Mayor of Albertville and my name is Mayor Edgar Feedbag.'

4. Assign roles and set the scene. Tell the characters what you expect of them. Please note:

   a. Invent creative restraints for any dangerous characters to avoid control problems.

   b. For younger students or for students not used to role play, I often eliminate the character of the boy in this role play. I find that sometimes when all the citizens start yelling at the boy, the student playing that character gets upset. Even though the student knows it is pretending, reality and fantasy get confused. So if my students haven't done a lot of role play, I simply say that the boy is locked in the Mayor's office until we can decide what we want to do with him.

   c. Do not let students use the names of classmates, the names of television or movie characters, or the names of television or movie settings in a role play. They need to think for themselves.

   d. Remember boys can pretend to be girls and vice-versa, but do not push this, if there's lots of resistance.

'*Now at this meeting I need some characters to join me up front in these chairs. I need the wolf, which we will keep in an imaginary cage. Who will be the wolf? Good. I need you to think about why the wolf attacked the sheep and how he's feeling after the attack.*

I'll need the boy. Let's come up with a name for him, and it can't be the name of anyone in this class or any name from television.

Okay, Billy it is. Who will play the boy, Billy? Anthony? Great! Anthony, I need you to think about why Billy played the trick on the citizens and how he is feeling now.

I'll need five wounded and hurt sheep. Who would like to pretend to be the sheep? Sheep, we need you to tell us what happened yesterday and how you are feeling today.

And the rest of the class will be the citizens of Albertville. How are you feeling? What do you want now? By the way, all of the animal characters can talk for the purposes of this role play.'

5. Have the students create name tags and/or a simple costume for their characters. They may want to use a small prop as well.

   Please note: Feel free to give time for the students to create a costume or let students get something out of a costume box or out of their lockers. If you assign roles the day before, each student could bring in a costume piece from home.

'Now, for those characters we haven't assigned names, I want you to create a name for yourself. Then I want everyone to write that name on these stick-on name tags. Write your imaginary name in big letters with these magic markers. Do not put your name tags on yet. I'll tell you when to put them on. Then I'm going to give you five minutes to make or find a costume piece that suits your character.'

6. Set up a clear beginning and end to the role play.

'Okay, everyone take your places. Wolf, come sit here. Remember, you are in an imaginary cage. Billy, our boy, you can sit over here . . . Now, everyone else clear your laps, desks, and hands of anything that is not going to be used in the role play. Now in a minute we'll close our eyes and when I count to three we won't be here—we will be in Albertville. When we open our eyes, we will put on our name tags, and the role play will begin. The role play will be over when I say "Citizens, thank you all for coming."'

7. Remind students of expectations, and give them permission to use their own creativity.

'Okay, close your eyes, close your eyes. When we open our eyes we'll be in Albertville. Think about what your character might want at this meeting. What is your character feeling and thinking? What does your character want the outcome of this meeting to be? How does your character look or sound? See if you can change your voice and body to sound and look like your character. Good, I think we are ready to go to Albertville. One . . . two . . . three . . . . Put on your name tags.'

8. Immediately become your character. Begin the role play by explaining its purpose, and then, through questions, illicit responses from the other characters.

'Ladies and gentlemen of Albertville, I, Mayor Feedbag, have called this meeting because something terrible happened yesterday! Many of you lost a lot of sheep yesterday, and I know you are upset. We're here today to find out what can be done about this.

Would any citizens like to tell us what's been going on these last few weeks and what happened yesterday? (Get responses.)

Billy, why did you do this? Why did you call "Wolf!" when there wasn't any? (Get response.) Billy, look out there— how do you think the citizens are feeling right now? (Get response.)

Sheep, what happened to you yesterday? Tell us your stories. (Get responses.) Wolf, what do you have to say for yourself? Why did you attack the sheep? How do you feel about what happened? Would you do it again? (Get response.)

(Please note: Usually the student playing the wolf simply says, "Because I was hungry, that's my nature, and of course I'll do it again." Expect that.)

'Well, citizens, you've heard their stories. Do you have any questions for anyone up here? (Get responses.)

What do you want to say to Billy? (Get responses.)

9. Resolve the problem if there is one to be resolved. Please note: Feel free to eliminate violence as an answer to the problem. Get a number of ideas. You may vote on several responses or combine ideas.

'So now, what should we do? What can we do together to solve this problem, and how can we make Billy understand what he did? By the way, you know we can't hurt Billy in any way. That's one of the laws here in Albertville. So what should we do?

What should we do with the wolf? Anything?

Well, citizens, I think we've come up with some fine answers here. I think we've done a very good job.'

10. Close the role play.

'Citizens, I want to thank you all for coming.

Close your eyes, close your eyes . . . because at the count of three we'll open our eyes, and take off our name tags, and give ourselves a hand. One . . . two . . . three . . . . Take off your name tags and give yourselves a hand—good job.'

11. Give special thanks to anyone who played a difficult character like the boy in this story and remind him or her that we were all just acting/pretending.

'You all did such a great job! And didn't Anthony do a good job pretending to be Billy? That was really a hard role to play with everyone yelling at him. You know that no one is really angry with you, Anthony—in fact we want to give you a special round of applause for doing such an excellent job in acting the role of Billy. Let's give Anthony a big hand.'

12. Feel free to summarize or discuss the results of the role play.

   '*So do you think the citizens did the right thing? Do you think Billy's punishment was fair? What do you think Billy learned from this experience? What did you learn?*'

Modifications

This structure can also be used for an historical event. I've used it for a variety of issues, such as: the colonists complaints against the British, Supreme Court segregation cases, and issues leading up to the Civil War.

Comments

See "Role Play, Lessons One and Three," "Acting Out a Story," "Continuing the Story," "Point of View Switch," and "Object Transformation/Playbuilding, Lessons Two and Three" for more ideas for role play and dramatization.

Personal Notes & Adaptations

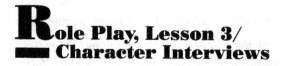

Role Play, Lesson 3/
▄ Character Interviews

Overview: Students transform into characters and are interviewed by the class

Objectives: To develop questioning skills
To review any subject
To promote creative thinking

Grade level: PreK to 6

Materials: Varies (Homemade microphone optional)

Group size: Small groups or entire class

Classroom setup: A circle or at desks, a clear space in front of the room

Procedure & Dialogue

1. Preset the class.

   ❛*Today we are going to pretend to be somebody else, and we are going to do that by using our imaginations.*❜

2. Have the students transform into another person, animal, or object. This can be done by using a suggestive costume piece or a large name tag or by the activities, "Imaginary Mask" or "Magic Hat."

   For older students, a costume piece or a large name tag works best. Here a large cardboard sign with a string loop that fits over the student's head and around the neck is used. The character being interviewed is Helen Keller for a grade three biography unit.

   ❛*We have just finished reading a biography of Helen Keller, and now I would like some of you to share with us what you learned about Helen Keller's life. I am going to ask you to do that by pretending to be Helen Keller.*

   You can see I've made this big cardboard name tag that will fit over your heads. I want one of you to come up here; I'll put the sign over your head and around your neck, and when I do, you will pretend to be Helen Keller. The rest of the class will then ask questions about your life.

   Oh, by the way, we know that Miss Keller is no longer alive and that when she was alive that she could not hear and had great difficulty speaking, but today, through the use of imagination, we will have the rare opportunity to hear her innermost thoughts and hear her speak.

When the first person is finished being Miss Keller, we will give someone else a turn. Who would like to go first? Anna, come up here.'

3. Have the student turn his or her back to the class while you put on the name tag or costume piece.

   'Okay, Anna. Now turn around, and I'm going to put this sign around your neck. When you face the class, if we are using our imaginations, we won't see Anna anymore; instead we'll meet Miss Helen Keller.'

4. Once the transformation has occurred, the class can interview the character. Always address the student who is pretending as the character.

   'Welcome Miss Keller. We are very honored to have you here. What questions do we want to ask Miss Keller? What would we like to know about her everyday life? What things could she now share with us that she may never have said before? What secrets or dreams did she have? What are we curious to know more about?'

5. Use the imaginary microphone while conducting the interview (see "Guidelines for Success").

   'Who has a question for Miss Keller? Yes, Ernesto, speak right into my microphone.'

6. After several questions, check to see if the student playing Miss Keller is getting uncomfortable or is struggling to answer. If so, simply thank the character, have the student turn their back to the class, lift the sign or remove the costume piece and then have the student face the class. Applaud the student. Then get another volunteer.

   'Miss Keller, thank you so much for coming. (Turn the student around). Let's see who is under that sign. (Student faces the class.) It's Anna! Let's give Anna a hand.'

7. Remind students that we are only pretending, so that boys can be girls and girls can be boys. The older the students the more resistant they are to this idea. But often there are a few students willing to break the ice. If you go first playing a character of the opposite sex, that usually helps. But if the class will not do this, do not force the issue.

   'Now who else would like to be Helen Keller? Remember, we are using our imaginations, so girls can pretend to be

boys, and boys can pretend to be girls. What boy would like to pretend to be Helen Keller? Good, Justin, come up to the front of the room.'

8. Repeat the process.

9. Close the activity.

'*You did a wonderful job pretending to be Helen Keller and interviewing her. I can see you all learned a lot about her over the past few weeks. Now close your eyes and relax, because we are done pretending, and it's time to return to the real world. One . . . two . . . three . . . Open your eyes.'*

Activity Variations for Older Students

1. Create a talk-show format in which a group of characters are interviewed (see "Point of View Switch").

2. Create a press conference. Have all the students bring costume pieces to turn themselves into news reporters. Have them interview the character(s) and then write a newspaper article based on the interview (see "Point of View Switch").

The students can turn into animate and inanimate objects. The sun and moon can be interviewed and share their jobs and unique qualities. Any character from history, literature, or current events can come to life (see the introduction to this chapter).

Comments

This is a great alternative to the written book report, or it can be used as a prewriting activity.

"Role Play, Lessons One and Two," "Acting Out a Story," "Continuing a Story," and "Point of View Switch" are good extensions of this activity.

Personal Notes & Adaptations

7

Literature Enrichment & Extension Activities
Story Dramatization

 Story dramatization is simply the process of acting out stories. The stories are ones the students have heard or have read.

Story dramatization enhances language, memory, and sequencing skills. The students act out the story in the proper sequence but often do so in their own words, using the book as a guide. This helps students internalize the story and thereby increases reading comprehension. Once the students have acted out a story they know, they can use higher-level thinking to extend the story and create their own scenarios.

This chapter includes several techniques for acting out stories as well as several strategies for extending story lines to create new stories.

The next chapter on playbuilding focuses on techniques that help students to create their own stories and then act them out. Obviously, there is some overlap between the two sections. It would be beneficial to read both sections before dramatizing stories with your class.

Story Can Theatre, Lesson 1

Overview: Students observe and/or participate in a story or lesson presented with small objects

Objectives: To strengthen sequencing, listening comprehension, and problem-solving skills

Grade level: Structure is appropriate for PreK to 6. This lesson is designed for PreK to 1. (For older students, see Activity Variations at the end of this lesson.)

Materials: A can, various miniature toys and objects

Group size: Small group or entire class

Classroom setup: A desk in front of the room as a stage, students on the floor or in chairs

Procedure & Dialogue

1. Select a theme or story you wish to present. Here the theme is spring planting for grades PreK to 1 (see "Story Can Theatre, Lessons Two, Three, and Four" for other lesson ideas).

2. Gather various miniature toys and objects to place in the coffee can that reflect the theme you've chosen. Create a story that uses all the objects. You may also use a book and simply act it out with miniatures. For the story on planting, the coffee can contains a toy farmer, a tractor, fruits and vegetables, a shovel, and the like.

3. Set a desk up in front of the class as a stage.

4. Preset the class. Let the students talk about the colors of the can. Have the students identify letters and words. Then shake the can. Have the students visualize what might be inside the can.

   '*What do I have in my hands? That's right, a coffee can. What color is the top of my can? What color is the side of my can? What letter is this? Can anyone tell me what this can says? Now I'm going to shake it. What do you think is in the can? Keys? What else? Candy? What else? Coins? Those are good guesses. Now I'll show you what's inside, and you're going to be so surprised!*'

5. Tell the story by removing the objects one by one from the can and placing them appropriately on your stage.

   '*Once upon a time there was a farmer named Artie (*take out the farmer) *and he went out in his fields on his tractor* *(take out tractor) to plant flower and fruit and vegetable seeds (pull out seeds).'*

6. If the story has repeating dialogue, the students can participate as the story unfolds.

   'What did Artie plant? Right—flower and fruit and vegetable seeds. Now one day . . .'

7. After the story, question the class to evaluate their listening and observation skills. Line the objects up, sequentially, based on how they came out of the can.

   'What object came out of the can first? What object came out second? . . . Now who remembers the name of the farmer? Good, Alexis. Come up and put Artie, the farmer, back in the can. What did he find in the ground with his shovel? Good, Becky. Put the basket in the can.'

8. Close the activity.

   'Well, all of my objects are back in the can. I'm going to put the lid back on my can because my story is over; now give yourselves a hand for being such good listeners.'

Activity Extensions

1. The next day, ask questions that facilitate the students in retelling the story.

2. Leave the can out for the children to play with. They will retell the story and create their own.

3. After telling the story several times, act it out (see "Acting Out a Story").

Activity Variations for Older Students, Grades 2 to 6

1. Coffee cans filled with miniatures can be given to small groups, and the students can create their own stories (see "Story Can Theatre, Lessons Three and Four").

2. Present a story that has no ending. Let the students predict outcomes and provide a solution (see "Story Can Theatre, Lesson Two").

3. Use the activity as an introduction to a story or set of characters. Then let the students use a part of the story

(characters, setting, and so on) to create another story (see "Story Can Theatre, Lesson Three").

4. Put three vocabulary words and three objects in the can. Have the students create sentences or a story using the words and the objects (see "Story Can Theatre, Lesson Four").

5. Have the students bring in three objects in a can, switch cans with a partner, and create a story with those objects up to the point of conflict. Then have the student present that story line to another student who must then resolve the conflict (see "Story Can Theatre, Lesson Four").

Comments

The miniatures really grab the students' attention.

Craft stores, thrift stores, flea markets, and catalogues are great sources for cheap miniatures.

See "Story Can Theatre, Lessons Two, Three, and Four" for more detailed examples for using this technique.

Personal Notes & Adaptations

Story Can Theatre, Lesson 2

"Lenny and the Ring of Fire," by Lenore Blank Kelner

Overview: Students observe and participate in a story presented with small miniature objects; students must supply the conclusion of the story

Objectives: To strengthen sequencing, listening, comprehension, and problem-solving skills

Grade level: PreK to 2

Materials: Place the following items in the coffee can in this order:

- One popsicle stick or broken chopstick

- One ring of fire (may be made of red and orange pipe cleaners; use your imagination)

- Lenny, the circus lion

- One trapeze artist (glue or securely fasten a tiny doll to a popsicle stick or a matchbox cover and attach pipe cleaners or string to make a swing)

- Two animals that look exactly alike (I use bears)

- Three or four elephants (it's best if they are different sizes, ranging from small to large)

- One ringmaster

- One set of plastic balloons

Group size: Small group or entire class

Classroom setup: A desk in the front of the room as a stage, students on the floor or in chairs

Procedure & Dialogue

1. Preset the class. Follow step 4 of "Story Can Theatre, Lesson One."

2. Tell the story outlined here. Try to change your voice when playing the ringmaster. It helps the students differentiate between you (the narrator) and the character of the ringmaster.

LENNY AND THE RING OF FIRE
A Story Can Theatre story by Lenore Blank Kelner

Open the can with a lot of excitement and an air of mystery. Take out the balloons and say:

NARRATOR: The balloons of the circus went up, up to the top of the circus tent and floated on down to the ground. And out came the ringmaster (take out the ringmaster) and he said . . .

RINGMASTER: Ladies and gentlemen, welcome, welcome to the circus! For our first act, in the center ring, we present the family of elephants! Let's give them a hand and count them as they enter the circus ring. (Have the students count the elephants as you pull them from the can.) One . . . two . . . three . . . four! There are four elephants: a big papa, a smaller mama, a big sister, and a baby brother. (If the elephants have distinguishing features, point them out. These can be good details for the students to recall in the extension section of the lesson. For instance you might say: The papa had long sharp tusks coming out of the side of his nose. The mama had a fluffy tail, and so on.)

NARRATOR: And they held each other's tails and walked all around the circus tent. And then the Mama jumped on the Papa's back (make a groaning noise). Then the sister jumped on the Mama's back (make a higher pitched groaning noise). Then the baby jumped on the big sister's back (make a high-pitched squeal of terror). And they made a great big tower, and everyone loved them and gave them a big hand.

ALL: (Applaud)

NARRATOR: Then the baby jumped off (squeal), the sister jumped off (groan), the Mama jumped off (lower groan), and then the Papa laid on his side, rolled over on his back and then rolled on his other side. Then he stood up and took a bow and made that great big noise Papa elephants make. Let's do it all together:

ALL: AHOW!

NARRATOR: Then the Mama took a bow, and she made the noise Mama elephants make. Let's do it together:

ALL: (Higher pitched) AHOW!

NARRATOR: Then the big sister took a bow and made the noise big sister elephants make. Let's do it together:

ALL: (Even higher pitched) AHOW!

NARRATOR: And then the baby took a bow and made the noise baby elephants make. Let's do it together:

ALL: (Extremely high pitched) AHOW!

NARRATOR: And everyone loved them and gave them a great big hand.

ALL: (Applaud)

RINGMASTER: And now ladies and gentlemen, for your entertainment—presenting the twin dancing bears Pete and Pat (take out bears). Let's give them a hand as they come into the circus ring.

NARRATOR: And out, out, out into the circus ring came Pete and Pat the twin dancing bears. They looked just alike on the outside—just the same. But on the inside they were very different. For you see, Pete liked spaghetti and Pat didn't like it at all. And Pete had a very loud voice and Pat was very quiet—but on the outside they looked the same. And the brothers danced (move the bears) and jumped (move the bears again). Then Pete did his big trick. He danced on his head and then jumped to his feet and then jumped way up high in the air (move the bear). And then Pat did his big trick. He did five flips. Let's count them (flip the bear).

ALL: One . . . two . . . three . . . four . . . five.

NARRATOR: And then the brothers hugged and kissed (move bears accordingly). And everyone loved Pete and Pat and gave them a big hand.

ALL: (Applaud)

RINGMASTER: And now, ladies and gentlemen, for your entertainment we present a very dangerous act! Up, up, up in the air will go the lady on the flying trapeze swing! This is a very dangerous act. She could fall off. We must be quiet, but first; let's give her a drum roll.

NARRATOR: Get out your drums everyone!

ALL: (Slap knees or in some way improvise drum sounds)

NARRATOR: (take out swing) And up, up, up high over the circus ring, sat the lady on her flying trapeze swing. And she swung back and forth and back and forth (swing toy) and everyone was so afraid she'd fall they all gasped:

ALL: Huhh! (cover your mouth)

NARRATOR: And then she did her big trick—the loop the loop! (Swing her very quickly over your head). She swung around and around so fast that everyone was so afraid she'd fall they all screamed:

ALL: AHHHH!!!

NARRATOR: But she didn't fall off her swing, and everyone loved her and gave her a great big hand!

ALL: (Applaud)

RINGMASTER: The lady on the flying trapeze, ladies and gentlemen! And now, ladies and gentlemen, the star of our circus and the most dangerous act of all. I present to you now Lenny, the circus lion, who will jump through the Ring of Fire. Drum roll please.

ALL: (Pretend to play drums)

NARRATOR: And out, out, out came Lenny, the beautiful and proud circus lion (take out lion). And out, out, out came the Ring of Fire (take out fire)! Well, Lenny was scared. He really wanted to go through the Ring of Fire—he really did but he was scared. He loved the circus! He wanted to be a good circus lion, but he was just too scared! He looked at everyone waiting for him to go; he knew he should, but he just couldn't do it. So he turned around and ran and hid in his cage (put Lenny back in the can).

And everyone who had come to see him go through the Ring of Fire was very disappointed. They all made sad faces. Let's do it together:

ALL: (Make sad faces)

NARRATOR: Well, that night after everyone went home, the Ringmaster came to Lenny's cage and he yelled . . .

RINGMASTER: Lenny!

NARRATOR: (Bring Lenny out of the can) And Lenny came to the front of his cage and the Ringmaster said . . .

RINGMASTER: Lenny, I paid you to jump through the Ring of Fire, and you didn't do it. Listen, Lenny, you'd better jump through that Ring tomorrow night, or you'll have to stay in your cage forever, and I know you don't want that! So Lenny, you'd better jump through that Ring of Fire!

NARRATOR: Well, Lenny didn't see but behind the Ringmaster's back he had a stick (take out stick) and he hit Lenny and he hit Lenny again. And Lenny cried and cried (touch Lenny's eyes as if to dry his tears). And then the Ringmaster walked away and came back and hit Lenny again.

RINGMASTER: So Lenny . . . you'd better jump through that ring tomorrow night!

NARRATOR: And Lenny cried and cried.

Storybuilding Section

This is where the scripted action stops, and you will need to facilitate the students in finishing the story and solving Lenny's problem.

NARRATOR: (Pet lion) Do you think it was a very good idea for the Ringmaster to hit Lenny? (get answers) Do you think it's a very good idea for anybody to hit anyone? (get answers) Well, that's why Lenny came here today, because he knew he was in trouble, and whenever you are in trouble, it's important to tell a friend. Will you be Lenny's friends?

For Kindergarten to Grade 2

NARRATOR: I think Lenny would like to talk right now, and this is the way he does it. If you hold Lenny in your hand and pretend to be Lenny, you can talk and tell us what Lenny is thinking. Who will hold Lenny and pretend to be Lenny and tell us what Lenny is thinking and feeling? (Put Lenny in the student's palm and direct your questions to Lenny. Look at the lion, not the student.)

What happened to you Lenny? Why did you get hit? Where do you hurt? How can we help you? (Let several students hold the lion and be Lenny and answer the questions. Often children will automatically change their voices as they take on the role of Lenny.)

For All Students

NARRATOR: Well, Lenny is feeling pretty sad right now. What can we do to cheer him up? Can we give him anything? Or say anything? (Take several answers, and let the students "give" him imaginary balloons or toys or whatever they wish.)

Lenny really liked everything you gave him. I think he'd like to get a hug or a pat, too. Who would like to hug or pet Lenny? (If the group can be patient, give everyone who wants to a turn.)

Problem-Solving Section

NARRATOR: Well Lenny is feeling a lot better right now, and he really wants to go through that Ring of Fire, but he's just so scared. How can we help him? (Get ideas from the students. Then try to incorporate as many ideas as you can into the end of the story. If they say, "Get water," then have the students imagine buckets or hoses next to them to spray Lenny as he goes through.

If they say, "Teach him", then have two students hold hands and create an imaginary Ring of Fire. Have another student jump through it holding Lenny.

If they say, "Kill the Ringmaster," tell the students that we said hitting and hurting weren't good ideas, but that maybe they can tell the Ringmaster with words just how angry they feel. Then bring the Ringmaster back, and let the students tell the Ringmaster how they're feeling. It helps to promote language if the Ringmaster is mean when he first addresses the students. If he says, "What do you want?" in an irritated voice, it provokes answers from the students. At the end of the conversation, have the Ringmaster apologize to Lenny.

Let the students dictate how the story will end.)

NARRATOR: What can we say to Lenny so he will feel strong and brave? (Get ideas) Well, let's see what happened the next night.

Incorporating Their Ideas

RINGMASTER: And now ladies and gentlemen, presenting Lenny, who will jump through the Ring of Fire! Drum roll, please!

ALL: (Pretend to play drums)

NARRATOR: And out, out, out came Lenny the beautiful and proud circus lion. And out, out, out came the Ring of Fire.

Well, Lenny was scared, but he remembered all the presents and hugs and pats he got. And he heard his friends saying (insert the words the students came up with to encourage Lenny). He remembered (include any ways the students devised to train him. For instance, "He remembered all the practice Kim and Angela gave him" or "He remembered he had on a fire-proof coat and so he was safe"). And so he . . . did it!! (If the students have water, have them throw it at the end.) And from that time on Lenny wasn't afraid, and he went through the Ring of Fire!

Give yourselves a hand for doing such a great job!

Activity Extensions

1. Assess listening skills. Have the students arrange the objects sequentially, based on how they came out of the can.

   '*Now let's see who is a good listener. I'm going to mix up everything I have here on the desk. I want to see who can tell me, when I started the story, what was the first thing I took out of the can? What came out next? . . . Last?*'

2. Have the students count and categorize the objects. You can even do some math.

   '*Let's count everything that came out of the can. How many animals came out? So how many things are left?*'

3. Have the students who come up answer a comprehension question and then place the object back in the can. (If possible, let each student have a turn. This gives you a chance to do some quick individual instruction. When you run out of objects, take the objects back out of the can so everyone can have a turn. Save your most active students for last. This gives them an incentive to sit still in order to get a turn.)

   '*Now if we can all be good friends and wait our turns, everyone can help me put my things back in the can. I'll ask four students to come up. Larry, Rosalie, Bonita, and Philip, will you come up? Larry, what would you like to put in my can? Choose something. What is that, Larry?*

   Right, it's the Ring of Fire. Who was afraid of the Ring? How did we help him? Rosalie, what do you want to put in the can?

   Let's give these children a hand. I need four more students.'

4. After all the students have had a turn, close the activity.

   '*You did a great job and now I'm going to put the lid back on my can because my story is over. Give yourselves one more hand.*'

5. Have the students retell the story the next day. Ask questions that promote memory and thinking skills.

   'What's going to come out of the can first? Right, the balloons. Where did they go? Yes, they went up, up, up, and then down to the ground. What came out next?'

6. Let the students play with the objects. They will retell the story and create new stories.

7. After telling the story several times, act it out (see "Acting Out a Story." *Lenny and the Ring of Fire* is the example used in that activity.)

Comments

It helps if you rehearse this story by yourself several times before you present it.

If the students cannot come up with any ideas for solving Lenny's problem, then you may want to suggest some and let the students choose one or two. You can also ask questions that promote problem solving, for instance, "What puts out fire?"

I have told this story over 300 times and I still am amazed by the creativity and thinking it promotes. I never know what the students will say.

This story is about finding an alternate solution to a problem other than violence. The students feel compassion for Lenny and want to help him. The gentleness this story evokes is often very moving.

You can use the structure of this lesson to create your own Story Can Theatre stories. Any book can be used in the same way. Read the book to the students (with or without the ending), and then tell the story with the toys. The students can orally compose their own ending to the story.

Personal Notes & Adaptations

Story Can Theatre, Lesson 3

"The Magical Tree," by Lenore Blank Kelner

Overview: Students observe and participate in a story presented with small miniatures. In this lesson students predict outcomes. Older students (grades two through six) can use the structure of the story to create their own Story Can Theatre stories.

Grade level: PreK to 6

Materials: Place the following toys and items in a coffee can in this order:

- a black piece of fabric to be used as mud

- some bees

- a rock

- a turtle

- a hippopotamus

- a zebra

- a rabbit

- an owl

- a tree decorated with all sorts of fruit

Group size: Small group or entire class

Classroom setup: A desk or small table in front of the room as a stage, students on the floor or in chairs.

Procedure & Dialogue

1. Follow step 4 of "Story Can Theatre, Lesson One."

2. Tell the story outlined here. Try to change your voice or your dialect for each animal. Rehearse the story by yourself several times in order to keep the voices consistent. Use your hands and face to extend the action and character reactions.

   Please note: The story here is written for young children (PreK through 2). However, with slight modification it works well with older students.

   It helps if you tell older students to watch carefully because they will be creating their own stories after the presentation.

THE MAGICAL TREE
by Lenore Blank Kelner
(Adapted from the story "The Tale of the Name
of the Tree," by Pattie Price)

NARRATOR: Hundreds and hundreds and hundreds and hundreds of years ago in Africa in the tall grasslands there was a (take the tree out of the can) tree. It was a magical tree. Now the reason this tree was magical is because all different kinds of fruits grew on one tree. Apples and pears and grapes and berries all grew on one tree. And that's not the way fruit grows. Usually we just have an orange tree or a pear tree, but on this tree all different kinds of fruit could be found. But do you know what? It was magical for another reason too. Because if you said the secret name of the tree, the fruit would fall and fall and fall and keep falling, and no one would ever be hungry again. Well, there was only one animal that knew the secret name of the tree and that animal was the wise old (hold up owl for younger children and wait for them to identify it) . . .

ALL: Owl!

NARRATOR: Right, an owl. The wise old owl knew the secret name of the magical tree and whenever someone asked her the name, this is what she said:

OWL: (Flap arms as wings) Hoo! Hoo! The name of the tree is Oo-wonga-lay-ma. Say the name and the fruit will fall. (Let your voice trail off, as if falling.)

NARRATOR: Let's be the owl together. Get your little wings out. Let's say what the owl said. Are you ready? Here we go. (Do not ask students in grades three through six to flap their wings. Just ask them to say the chant.)

ALL: Hoo! Hoo! The name of the tree is Oo-wonga-lay-ma. Say the name and the fruit will fall.

NARRATOR: Let's do it again. Get your wings out. Here we go.

ALL: Hoo! Hoo! The name of the tree is Oo-wonga-lay-ma. Say the name and the fruit will fall. (Students in grades three through six do not need to repeat the chant.)

NARRATOR: Well, one summer it was very, very hot. The sun was shining very brightly on the land. But there was no rain, so nothing grew on the land and the animals were very, very hungry. There was no food for them to eat. (For students in grades four through six, you may want to add the phrase: There was a famine in the land. See if they know the definition of famine.) But four animal friends remembered about the magical tree and they came to the magical tree. The four animal friends that came to the tree were a . . . (hold up the rabbit)

ALL: Rabbit!

NARRATOR: Right! A rabbit. A . . . (hold up the zebra)

ALL: Zebra!

NARRATOR: Good! A zebra. Now the other animal that came to the magical tree was a . . . (hold up the hippo)

ALL: Hippopotamus!

NARRATOR: Good! Let's say it together.

ALL: Hippopotamus.

NARRATOR: (For younger children) Sometimes we call them hippos. Let's say it one more time.

ALL: Hippopotamus.

NARRATOR: And there was one more animal that came to the magical tree (hold up the turtle).

ALL: A turtle! (Students in grades two through six do not need to identify the animals. Make this section more presentational; just present the animals and move on with the story.)

NARRATOR: A turtle. Good! The four animal friends that came to the magical tree were a bunny rabbit, a zebra, a hippopotamus, and a turtle. But uh-oh. They got to the tree, and they realized that none of them knew the secret name of the tree. And without the secret name, the fruit would not fall.

RABBIT: (Pick up each animal as they talk.) TTT . . . What are we going to do? TTT . . . What are we going to do? None of us know the name of the tree. TTT . . . And without the name of the tree the fruit will not fall.

ZEBRA: Oh my dear. This is terrible. Why, none of us know the name of the tree. What are we going to do?

HIPPO: Hey! Hey! This is really bad. This is terrible. 'Cause I gotta tell you something—I'm a big guy. I gotta eat something, and I gotta eat something quick. What are we going to do?

TURTLE: Oh, this is terrible. I'm so hungry. What are we going to do?

ZEBRA: Oh my dear. I just remembered something. There is a wise old owl that lives deep, deep, deep inside the grasslands. All we have to do is find the wise old owl, ask her for the name of the tree. She'll tell us, we'll come back, say the name, the fruit will fall, and we won't be hungry anymore. What do you think about that?

HIPPO: Hey! Hey! That is a great idea, Zebra. Great idea. We gotta get to that owl, and we gotta get to that owl quick! So it's gotta be one of you fast animals—like you bunny rabbit or the zebra 'cause it would take me a long time. I'm a big guy so I'm kinda slow. But, speaking of slow, the turtle here, the turtle's so slow, by the time he gets back, we'll all be starving. (Laughs) What a slowpoke you are, turtle! (Laughs again) So who's it gonna be? You, bunny rabbit or the zeeb.

RABBIT: I'll go.

NARRATOR: And so the rabbit raced through the grasslands and over the mountain to the wise old owl. Now every time I say grasslands, I want you to rub your hands together to make the sound of our feet walking in tall grass. Let's try it. And so the rabbit raced through the grasslands (pause and do motion) and over the mountain to the wise old owl. (Students in grades two through six need not do the grassland noise.)

RABBIT: TTT . . . Wise old owl? Wise old owl? TTT . . . We're very, very, very hungry. Do you think you could give me the name of the magical tree? I'll go back, and TTT . . . I'll say it, and the fruit will fall, and we won't be hungry anymore. TTT . . .

NARRATOR: And the wise old owl said what she always said. Let's say it together. Get your little wings out.

ALL: Hoo! Hoo! The name of the tree is Oo-wonga-lay-ma. Say the name and the fruit will fall.

RABBIT: TTT . . . Thank you very much. TTT . . . Thank you very much. I must get back now to my friends. TTT . . .

NARRATOR: And so that rabbit raced back over the mountain and through the grasslands (pause for their motion) back, back to her friends. But uh-oh. The rabbit was going so fast that the rabbit was not looking where she was going and the rabbit fell right on a rock (take out the rock). Ah! And hurt her ear. Ah! And her ear hurt so much, that is all she could think about. And when she came back to her friends, she had forgotten the name of the magical tree.

RABBIT: TTT . . . Friends, I was going really fast. And I fell on a rock, and I hurt my ear. TTT . . . And I'm sorry, but I forgot the name of the magical tree. Oh! TTT . . . My ear hurts. I want my mommy. TTT . . .

ZEBRA: Oh my dear, then it looks like I'll have to go.

NARRATOR: And so that zebra zoomed through the grasslands (pause and do motion) and over the mountain to the wise old owl.

ZEBRA: Oh my dear wise old owl, could you help me out, old girl? You see, the rabbit forgot the name of the tree. Could you please give it to me? I'll take it back, say the name, the fruit will fall, and we'll be so grateful to you, my dear. Could you help me out, old girl?

NARRATOR: And the wise old owl said what she always said. Let's get our wings out and say it.

ALL: Hoo! Hoo! The name of the tree is Oo-wonga-lay-ma. Say the name and the fruit will fall.

ZEBRA: Oh my dear, thank you so very much. I must get back now to my friends.

NARRATOR: And so that zebra zoomed over the mountain and through the grasslands (pause and do motion) back, back to her friends.

ZEBRA: Oh my dear, is that the rock that got my friend the rabbit? Well, it's not going to get me, oh no, no, no. I'll just jump right over it. There I go.

NARRATOR: But the zebra, too, was going very fast. And the zebra, too, was not looking where she was going. And the zebra ran straight into a hive of bees (take out bees). And the bees stung her on the head, and the bees stung her on the side, and the bees stung her on the tail, and the bees stung her on the legs, and the bees stung her all over. And by the time that zebra came back to her friends, she was so bitten by the bees that she forgot the name of the magical tree.

ZEBRA: Oh my dear friends. Ow Ow Ow Ow Ow! Ow Ow the bees, the bees. Ow they stung me everywhere. I'm sorry to report, but I forgot the name of the magical tree. AY, EE, II, OOO, UUU, Ahh!!

HIPPO: Hey Hey! This is bad. This is terrible because now I gotta go and I'm not so fast. But I'll tell you something, I'm gonna go as fast as I can 'cause I got to eat.

NARRATOR: And so that hippopotamus heaved his way through the grasslands (pause and do motion) and over the mountain to the wise old owl.

HIPPO: Hey, Hey, Hey, wise old owl. I gotta apologize. The rabbit, the zebra, none of them guys can remember the name of that tree. Could you please give it to me and give it to me, quick 'cause I got to eat!

NARRATOR: And the wise old owl said what she always said. Let's say it together.

ALL: Hoo! Hoo! The name of the tree is Oo-wonga-lay-ma. Say the name and the fruit will fall.

HIPPO: Hey, Hey, Hey, thanks a million. Thanks a million. I gotta get back now to my friends.

NARRATOR: And so that hippopotamus heaved his way over the mountain and through the grasslands (pause and do motion) back, back to his friends.

HIPPO: Hey! There's that rock there that got my friend the rabbit. Hey rock, you're not gonna get me. I'll just stomp right over you. Ooo Ooo there're those bees there that got my friend the zebra. Hey bees, buzz off! You're not gonna get me. You know why? 'Cause my mom told me if you don't bother bees, they don't bother you, so I'm gettin' outta here. That's what I'm doin'. I'm gettin' out of here.

NARRATOR: Well, the hippopotamus went just a little bit further and the hippopotamus saw some wonderful mud (take out the mud). And the hippopotamus just loved the mud.

HIPPO: Ey, check it out. Mud. Ooh, I love the mud. I think I'll jump in it. Hey, that's great. I think I'm gonna roll in the mud. Whoa, that's just wonderful. I think I'll dance in it. Yeah!! You know what? I think I'm gonna take a little nap right here in the mud.

Predicting Section

NARRATOR: What do you think is going to happen when the hippopotamus wakes up? (Let the students predict what will happen to the hippo.) How do you think the story will end? (If possible, include a few of their ideas as you end the story or use their ideas instead of the ending written here.)

NARRATOR: Let's see what happens. Are you ready? Here we go.

HIPPO: That was a great nap. I think I'll just go back now to my friends and say the name of the . . . Oh no. Oh no. No. Not me too. Oh no no no. Oh no. Animal friends! Animal friends! I took a nap in the mud and woke up, and I forgot the name of the tree. Oh no! Turtle! Turtle! Look, I'm sorry I called you slow poke. I'm sorry I called you names and laughed at you. Turtle, go get the name of that tree. You're the only hope we got.

TURTLE: Oh Oh! I'll do the very best I can.

NARRATOR: And so the turtle trudged through the grasslands (pause and do motion) and over the mountain to the wise old owl.

TURTLE: Oh wise old owl, wise old owl. It's terrible. None of my friends can remember the name of the tree. How can I remember something I just have to remember?

OWL: Well, the best way to remember something, Turtle, is to ask the person to say it many times and then never stop saying it.

TURTLE: Oh, then please wise old owl, please give me the name of the magical tree.

ALL: Hoo! Hoo! The name of the tree is Oo-wonga-lay-ma. Say the name and the fruit will fall.

TURTLE: Oh, um, I don't want to bother you or anything, but it would help me a lot if you would say that again.

ALL: Hoo! Hoo! The name of the tree is Oo-wonga-lay-ma. Say the name and the fruit will fall.

TURTLE: Um, I don't want to be a pest. Please don't get mad or laugh at me or call me a name, but it would help me a lot if you could say it one last time.

ALL: Hoo! Hoo! The name of the tree is Oo-wonga-lay-ma. Say the name and the fruit will fall.

TURTLE: Oh, thank you, thank you very much. I must get back now to my friends.

NARRATOR: And so the turtle trudged over the mountain and through the grasslands (pause and do motion) back, back to his friends, saying the name of the tree the entire way home.

TURTLE: (Often the students join in and do the chant spontaneously.) The name of the tree is Oo-wonga-lay-ma. Say the name and the fruit will fall. The name of the tree is Oo-wonga-lay-ma . . .

Turtle: Oh no, there's that rock that got my friend the rabbit. Well, it's not gonna get me. No, I'm just gonna try to climb over it. Oh, I hope I can. Let me see. (Sigh) I did it. The name of the tree is Oo-wonga-lay-ma . . .

Oh no. There are those bees that got my friend the zebra. I'm not going to bother them and maybe they won't bother me. The name of the tree is Oo-wonga-lay-ma . . .

Oh no, what's this? The mud. Oh, I hope I won't fall asleep like the hippo. I'm just going to tiptoe right across. Please . . . let . . . me . . . get . . . through. Please . . . please . . . please . . . Whew!

The name of the tree is Oo-wonga-lay-ma. Say the name and the fruit will fall. The name of the tree is Oo-wonga-lay-ma. Say the name and the fruit will fall. Animal friends! Animal friends! I'm back, I'm back, and I think I have it now. I think I do. Let me think now!

Narrator: (Whisper) Let's say it together.

All: The name of the tree is Oo-wonga-lay-ma. (Let your voice really fall as the tree goes down to the desk.)

Narrator: And the fruit fell and fell, and the animals ate and ate, and they were hungry no more. And all of the animals clapped and cheered for the turtle. Let's give him a hand. And that's the story of the four animal friends and the magical tree. You did a very good job listening. Now give yourselves a hand.

Activity Extensions

1. See Activity Extensions 1 to 7 in "Story Can Theatre, Lesson Two."

Activity Variations for Older Students, Grades 2 to 6

1. Put a story chart on the board for the students to fill out. Include on the chart: characters, setting, problem, solution, obstacles. After the students fill out the chart for this story, break the students into groups. Have each group write their own story using the same characters and setting but a different problem, solution, and obstacles. They can compose these stories in oral or written form. They can also rehearse and present them in a Story Can Theatre format to the group.

Feel free to vary this structure. For instance, you can put these characters in another setting or just have them create a different solution.

2. Use this as an introductory lesson for a unit on African folktales. Have the students work in pairs or groups to present their own African folktale in a Story Can Theatre format.

Comments

Be sure students rehearse before they present the story in a Story Can Theatre format in front of the class. Also encourage every member to speak at least once during the presentation. This stops a few students from taking over. At times students ramble on and on. You may just want them to present one key scene in front of the class.

As in "Story Can Theatre, Lesson Two," feel free to use this lesson as a guide to create your own. Students really enjoy this technique. They like to manipulate the objects and take on new voices. In a prewriting activity, I observed low-ability eighth-grade boys manipulate toys and speak as characters in a similar manner to PreK children. As a result of this oral composing technique, those students wrote more on paper than they had previously written all year.

I can't say enough about this strategy. I have literally hundreds of Story Can Theatre lessons.

Personal Notes & Adaptations

Story Can Theatre, Lesson 4

Overview: Miniature toys and several vocabulary words are placed in a can; students create sentences, paragraphs, or a story using words and objects

Objectives: To develop vocabulary
To promote creativity and language

Grade level: 2 to 6

Materials: A coffee can, miniature toys, index cards

Group size: Small groups or the entire class

Classroom setup: At desks

Procedure & Dialogue

1. Write three vocabulary words on a 3x5-inch index card. Place the card in a coffee can. Also place in the can three miniature toys. The toys do not have to have any relationship to each other or to the words on the card. Create enough cans for the students to work individually, in pairs or in groups. Keep in mind the students can bring in the can and the toys and can write the words on the cards. If you do this, have the students exchange cans rather than keep their own.

2. Ask the students to open the can and create three sentences, each using one of the objects and one of the vocabulary words. You may want to ask higher-level students to create a paragraph or a story using all three words and objects.

    'On your desk is a can. In the can are three of our new vocabulary words and three objects. I want you to write three sentences. In each sentence you are to use one object and one vocabulary word. Be sure you use the word accurately in the sentence. Check the definition if you are not certain you know what the word means.

    (Or) I want you to write a story using all three words and all three objects.'

Modifications

If you are studying a particular kind of literature, you may want to add that layer to this activity. For instance, ask the students to create a fairy tale, a folk tale, or a mystery story. In one class, the students were studying conflict, and so they were asked to write a story line up to the point that the conflict was clearly defined.

Some students cannot cooperate well enough to write stories as a group. If that is the case, have the students write individual stories or sentences, but all members of the group use the same words and the same objects as a springboard for their writing. If you do this, have the members of the group read their writing to each other. The students enjoy hearing how each group member used the same words and objects in a different way.

If the students just write sentences, you can have the students exchange cans in order to write more sentences.

Comments

This activity works well with all students. You may find the students play with the toys first and then start to write. Don't be troubled by this. They are orally composing. They will get down to putting their thoughts on paper. You will find this a fascinating process to observe.

Personal Notes & Adaptations

Random Vocabulary Story

Overview: Students use their vocabulary list as a stimulus for storybuilding.

Objective: To reinforce vocabulary words
To stimulate creativity

Grade level: 1 to 6

Materials: Five to ten words

Group size: Small group or entire class

Classroom setup: At desks or in small groups

Procedure & Dialogue

1. Select five to ten vocabulary words from which to work. It is best if they are unrelated words.

2. Place these on the board.

3. Choose one word with which to start and provide a beginning sentence using that word.

   '*"The octopus wrapped its tentacles around the rusty box."* That's the beginning sentence.'

4. Students must then orally or in writing create a story (or a play) using five of the vocabulary words. Students must use the words accurately in the story. They must start the story with your sentence.

   '*I want you to use that as the first sentence in a story you write. In your story you must use five of the other vocabulary words I've written here on the board. Be sure to use the words correctly. Check the definitions if you are not sure of the meanings of the words.*'

5. The students can share their stories, act key scenes out in groups, or illustrate them.

Optional

You may not want to give students a starting sentence. Simply tell them to create their own story with five vocabulary words.

The Creative Classroom

Activity Variations

This can be extended to reinforce opposites, rhyming words, math words, color words, and so on.

In order to increase vocabulary development further, the list of words may include: an adjective, an adverb, a proper noun, a common noun, a verb, and so on. The students can label each word and use it correctly in their sentence or story.

Comments

My fifth-grade teacher did this activity with my class many years ago. I remember it well. It prompted me to write a novel, which I continued to write for two years.

Personal Notes & Adaptations

Becoming Objects (A Variation of "Bits 'n' Pieces")

Overview: Students become objects in a particular location and create a scenario using those objects

Objectives: To explore a particular environment
To examine the parts of a whole
To create an original story

Grade level: PreK to 6

Materials: None

Group size: Small group or entire class

Classroom setup: A clear space, a circle

Procedure & Dialogue

1. Preset the class.

   'Are you ready to pretend and use your imaginations today? Good.'

2. Select a familiar location for the students to explore. Here the location is a kitchen for grades PreK through two and ESL students.

3. Explain to the class that they are going to set up their own kitchen, but that they are going to become all the objects found in the kitchen. Then they are going to create a story using those objects.

   'We're going to set up our own kitchen today, but instead of using real objects we're going to become those objects ourselves by using our bodies. Then we're going to write a story using all of the objects.'

4. Identify five or six items you might find in that location, and have the students create those objects with their bodies. Elicit ideas from the students as to how they can create the objects, and then embellish on their ideas.

   'What objects might we find in a kitchen? Paula? A sink. How could we use our bodies to create a sink? It looks like Paula is using her hands to create the hot and cold water faucets. What other part of the sink do we need?

   Yes, the basin and the pipes. Alex and Timmy, will you be our basin? Emily, can you be the pipe? That's good, Emily, lie down and attach yourself to the wall. What else do we want in our kitchen?

A refrigerator. Leah, how can you make yourself look like a refrigerator? I like how your fist is the door handle. Let's see if the light goes on when I open the door. Great, when the door opens, look at Leah smiling as if her face was the light. I like that a lot.'

5. You may want to let the students relax in their place after they have shown you their objects. It will be hard for them to keep up a pose for a long time (see "Statues One and Two").

   '*Paula, Alex, Timmy, Emily, and Leah, you can relax for a minute until we get the rest of our kitchen set up, but stay right in your places.'*

6. Create a story line using all of the objects.

   '*Okay, we have a sink, a refrigerator, a broom, a stove, and a rug. What could happen in this kitchen that would use these five things?*

   Somebody fell on the rug? Why?

   Because something fell out of the refrigerator and spilled on the floor.

   What spilled, Paul?

   (Student) *Milk. The mom filled her coffee pot in the sink and put it on the stove. She went to get the cereal and the milk fell out of the refrigerator. The milk spilled on the rug. She slipped and fell on the milk, and the cereal went flying all over the place.*

   (Teacher) *So then what happened? I see she cried, yelled for her kids, and they came and swept up the mess with the broom.*

   Sounds good. Let's do it.'

7. Assign roles, and act out the story (see "Acting Out a Story"). Feel free to add more objects.

   '*In our story we added two more objects—what were they? Right, the cereal and the milk. Who would like to be the cereal? Who would like to be the milk?'*

8. After the students build one story, they can create a second story in the same environment using the same or different objects.

9. Close the activity.

'*Great job! Now everyone go back and sit down at your desks. You did a wonderful job using your imaginations today. Now it's time to stop using our imaginations for acting, and start using them to write the story we just wrote. So take out a sheet of paper . . .*'

Activity Variation

1. Use this activity in connection with any other story dramatization or playbuilding activity. As students act out a story from literature or one they create, have them act out several or all of the objects in the story.

For Older Students, Grades 3 to 6

1. Break the students into groups and have them create a story that uses three or four objects, or have them act out part of a story they have read using people as objects. Students could also act out objects they associate with a particular country, culture, story, or time period.

For ESL Students

Modify the activity to review vocabulary about objects found in a particular room or location.

Personal Notes & Adaptations

Bits 'n' Pieces (A Variation of "Becoming Objects")

Overview: Students recreate an environment by transforming into all of its parts

Objectives: To explore a particular environment
To examine the parts of a whole

Grade level: PreK to 6

Materials: None

Group size: Small groups or entire class

Classroom setup: A circle or a clear space in front of the room

Procedure & Dialogue

1. Preset the class.

2. Select a location or environment. Here the location is an aquarium.

   '*Since we've just finished studying about our aquarium, today we are going to create the inside of our aquarium right here in front of the class. Of course, in order to do this we will have to pretend and use or imaginations.*'

3. Ask students to think of what is found in an aquarium. When a student has an idea, have the student act it out, and have the other students guess what it is.

   '*Think about what we can find in an aquarium. When you have an idea, I want you to come up and act out that idea. Okay, Lewis, start us off. What do you think he's become? A fish. Good Lewis, keep swimming. Let's really see you look and move like one of our fish.*'

4. Select students, one by one, to come up and add one more piece to the environment until it has been recreated. Coach the students to help their actions be more realistic and believable.

   '*Who has another idea? Tiara, come up and act out your idea. What does it look like Tiara is doing? Yes, I think she is the filter, too. Let's hear that filter, too, Tiara. What else do we need?*

   Al, go on up. What do you think he is? Yes, he does look like a piece of algae. I wonder if that fish eats algae?'

5. Select a class photographer to take an imaginary picture of the environment. This makes all the students concentrate and focus so that the location can really be observed by the class.

   'I think we've got a great aquarium here. Alice, take your imaginary camera and get a picture of it. Everyone really be in that world now, so Alice can get a good picture.'

6. Tell the students to relax and sit. Choose another location.

   'Good job. Now let's give them a hand. All right you can sit down. Now let's create another environment. We've been reading Native American stories from Alaska. Let's create the inside of a Native American community house. What does it look like?'

7. Close the activity.

   'I hope you enjoyed this activity. I certainly did. Now I need you to close your eyes for a moment because we have to stop pretending now and line up for lunch. One . . . two . . . three. Open your eyes.'

Activity Variations

1. This activity can be used in connection with any process as well, *e.g.*, the growing process, electricity, photosynthesis, or the life cycle or habitat of various plants and animals.

2. This activity can be used with large objects, *e.g.*, planes, trucks, or fire equipment, with the students becoming different parts of the object (see "Becoming Objects").

3. "Bits 'n' Pieces" can be adapted to fit a setting in a story or book.

Personal Notes & Adaptations

Imaginary Letter Writing

Overview: Students compose an imaginary letter to a real or fictional person

Objectives: To promote language and thinking skills
To compose a letter

Grade level: PreK to 1

Materials: None

Group size: Entire class

Classroom setup: At desks

Procedure & Dialogue

1. Select a real or imaginary person to whom the children can write. This person may be a character in a story, a holiday character, the grandmother in "Grandmother's Trunk," or a character that was developed through "Magic Hat," or "Story Can Theatre." Here the character for grades PreK to one is Gregory, the goat, from the book *Gregory, The Terrible Eater*, by Mitchell Sharmat.

2. Preset the class.

   ʻ*Today we are going to write an imaginary letter to our friend, Gregory, the goat, from the book* Gregory, The Terrible Eater.ʼ

3. Take the students step by step through the letter-writing process. Be sure to "write" right along with your students.

   Optional: You may really want to write their ideas on the board or on chart paper as they write on their imaginary paper. Doing this will help you if you choose to do Optional Ending 2 or 3 of this activity.

   ʻ*Are you ready? Good. Then if we are going to write a letter to Gregory, what do we need?*

   Right, paper and pencil. Let's reach behind us and find a piece of imaginary paper and an imaginary pencil. What else will we need?

   Right, an envelope and a stamp. Let's open the drawer in front of us and find them. Will we need anything else?

   Gregory's address. Where do you think he lives? You are right, we don't know. So how could we get the letter to him? We could send it to Dr. Ram and ask him to give it to Gregory. So let's write on our envelope: Gregory, the goat, c/o Dr. Ram.

What's Dr. Ram's address? Let's make one up: Goat Medical Center, Farmland, Pennsylvania.'

4. Ask the students questions that facilitate the creation of their letter.

'What do we want to say to Gregory? What questions do we have for him? Why didn't you like to eat goat food? Let's write that.

Did you really think you were a pig? Let's write it. . .'

5. Close the letter.

'I think we've written Gregory a terrific letter. How shall we sign it? Now what should we do with it?

So let's fold it and put it in the envelope, seal it, and put our stamp on it. Now what should we do?

Right, we need to mail the letter.'

6. Use "Magic Hat" or a costume piece to turn a student into a mail carrier (see the introduction to Chapter 6, "Role Play"). Here a real hat and bag are used.

Please note: You can also use a puppet as the mail carrier (see "The Shape Game").

'Well, who would like to put on this mail carrier's hat, and take this big bag, and pretend to be a mail carrier? Francesca, come up.

Who is this really?

Right, Francesca. But when she puts on this hat, who will she pretend to be? A mail carrier named . . . What should we name her?

She'll be a mail carrier named Mrs. Stamp. Turn around, Francesca.'

7. Put on the costume while the student has his or her back to the class.

'Oh, Mrs. Stamp, Mrs. Stamp! We need you!'

8. When the student faces the class, he or she speaks to the class as the character. Feel free to interview the character.

'Hello, Mrs. Stamp. Let's say "Hi" to Mrs. Stamp. Have you delivered a lot of mail today? Where have you been? How many letters have you delivered? Does anyone have any questions for Mrs. Stamp?'

9. Have the student explain why you need the mail carrier.

   'Who will tell Mrs. Stamp why we asked her here today? So, will you collect our letters and deliver them? Thank you.'

10. *Optional Ending 1:* You can close the activity here by having the mail carrier become him- or herself again.

    'Thank you, Mrs. Stamp (student turns his or her back to the class and teacher removes the costume). *Let's see who this really is? It's Francesca! Let's give her a hand.'*

11. *Optional Ending 2:* Have the mail carrier return with an imaginary letter from Gregory that the students take turns "reading." If you wrote their earlier ideas on the board, use them to guide the reading of the letter or see how well the students recall their questions.

    'Here comes Mrs. Stamp. It looks like she has a letter for us. What do you have for us today, Mrs. Stamp? A letter from Gregory! Great.

    Who will read the letter to the class? What else did he say? Who else will read the letter?'

12. *Optional Ending 3:* Transform another student into the character who receives the letter (see "Magic Hat" and the introduction to Chapter 6, "Role Play"). Have the mail carrier deliver the letter to him or her. Then let the class "listen" as the character writes back.

    Close the activity with the mail carrier delivering the answer to the class. The students can then "read" the letter again.

    Please note: If you decide to do this ending, you may want to become the mail carrier yourself. In that role you will better be able to facilitate the recipient of the letter to read and respond to the note. You can ask questions and remind him or her of the contents of the letter.

13. Close the activity.

    'You've done a great job using your imaginations. But now let's close our eyes and at the count of three, Gregory and the mail carrier and our letters will all be gone, and we'll be ourselves again. One . . . two . . . three.'

Comments

This is a good prewriting and composing activity for students who are learning to write a letter.

If you have been studying the postal system, feel free to include questions to the mail carrier that review appropriate information.

This activity can be extended over several days. On the first day they could write the letter and the next day they could receive a response. They may even want to write back a second time.

Personal Notes & Adaptations

Acting Out a Story (Story Dramatization)

Overview: Students act out a story

Objectives: To reinforce reading comprehension
To enhance language, sequencing, and memory skills

Grade level: PreK to 6

Materials: A story

Group size: Small group or entire class

Classroom setup: A circle or a clear space in the front of the room

Procedure & Dialogue

1. Read or tell a story to your students.

2. Review the sequence of the story. Here the example will be the "Story Can Theatre" story, *Lenny the Lion* (see "Story Can Theatre, Lesson Two").

   a. For younger students: You may want to use visual cues, *i.e.* pictures, miniatures, or toys, to remind them of the sequence.

      '*I hope you enjoyed that story. Now when I started the story, what came out of the can first? Right, the balloons. I'll put the balloons over here. Then what came out? Right, the Ringmaster. What did he say? "Ladies and Gentlemen, welcome, welcome to the circus!" I'll put the Ringmaster next to the balloons.*

      What animals performed first for the audience?'

   b. For older students: You may want to put key words on the board to remind them of the sequence. Use these visual reminders later to guide the story dramatization.

      '*What was the first thing that happened in our story? Right, the balloons floated up to the top of the circus tent. I'll write balloons here on the board. Then what happened? Right, the Ringmaster introduced the elephants. I'll write down Ringmaster/elephants. Then what happened?*'

3. Explain to the students that you want them to act out this story together.

'Now what we're going to do is act out this story. We are going to pretend to be all the parts and bring the story to life.'

4. Create a clear space in the room so that the students have room to move and to see each other. I often try to keep the students in a circle so everyone can see all the action.

'So let's push our desks back and stand in a big circle.'

5. Create a control device that will help you stop the action when necessary and also change the scene. Eventually, as the children understand what is expected of them and as they look forward to the process, you will need to use the control device less and less.

'Now whenever I say FREEZE! (clap my hands, beat this drum, or the like) I need you to stop whatever you are doing and listen, because it's time for us to change the scene or become different characters in our play.'

6. Practice this control device in a positive and fun way.

'So let's see if you can do it. Shake your bodies, shake everything, keep shaking —FREEZE! Good, relax . . . we have some good listeners today. Let's try it again. Shake, shake, shake, keep moving fingers, toes, head, neck— FREEZE! Good. Now relax. I think you've got it!'

7. Act with the children. In the beginning they will need you to model the action for them. Later they can lead their own dramatizations. As much as possible, involve all the students in the action. Try to avoid having stars. Have the entire class create the settings, say important or repeating lines, and create sound effects. For some stories, everyone can be the lead character. As the children become more comfortable with story dramatization, you can assign individual roles. But remember, creative drama is process- not product-centered. We want as many children taking creative risks as possible. Also if all the children are involved, they will be less competitive for parts.

'Let's begin. What's the first thing we are going to be in the story? Let's look over here at the board and see what came first. Right, the balloons. So let's all be the balloons. How can we make our bodies look like balloons? What did the balloons do?

Right, they went up, up, up to the top of the tent and floated on down to the ground—so let's do it. FREEZE! Then what happened? Right, the Ringmaster came out. Let's put on an imaginary black top hat and say what he said together:

*"Ladies and Gentlemen, welcome, welcome to the circus."
Then what did he say? Good. Let's say it. "Here's the family
of elephants." FREEZE!*

*Let's take off our top hats and be the elephants. What did
the elephants do? Right, they got on each other's backs.
How can we show that without hurting anyone?*

Version 1 (everyone in role): *Let's all be the elephants.
Show me what you can do with your bodies to look like
elephants. Let me hear the papa, the mama . . . Let's put
our trunk on a friend's back and pretend we are making the
tower of elephants . . .*

Version 2 (individuals in role): *How many children do we
need to be the family of elephants? Let's get a tall boy and
girl to be papa and mama and two shorter children for the
big sister and baby. Can you do something with your bodies to look like elephants? Now put your trunk on each
other's back and make your tower . . .'*

8. Ask questions to promote creativity, thinking, and language.

9. Allow the children to use their own language to tell the
   story.

10. In your first few story dramatizations, you may need to
    direct most of the action. As the children become more and
    more comfortable, let them narrate and provide suggestions
    for how to act out parts of the story.

11. Dramatize the same story several times either on the same
    day or over consecutive days. This helps to smooth out the
    process. The story will flow and you will not need to stop
    to ask as many questions or to "freeze" the action.
    Repetition reinforces the story line, allows different children
    to risk and take on key roles, and lets the children take over
    the process.

    *'Wonderful job! Let's act it out one more time and let's
    have different children be the elephants and Lenny.
    Tomorrow we'll do the story again.'*

12. Close the activity.

    *'You did a great job acting out our story. Give yourselves a
    hand. I'm looking forward to doing this again tomorrow.'*

Modifications

You may want to add some suggestive props or costumes for
the story.

Activity Variations

1. Read a story to the children, but do not read the end of the story. Let the children predict various endings to the story and act out several endings. Then read the written ending. Have the children discuss differences and preferences.

2. Have the children act out only key scenes or their favorite scenes in a story.

3. To reinforce the main elements of a story, have the students only act out the beginning, climax, and resolution of the story.

4. To reinforce the concept of conflict, have the students just act out the conflict in the story.

5. Have the students create another story using the same characters with a new problem.

6. See "Object Transformation/Playbuilding, Lessons Two and Three" as extension activities.

Comments

Read "Role Play, Lessons One, Two and Three," "Continuing a Story," "Point of View Switch," and "Object Transformation/ Playbuilding, Lessons Two and Three" before doing this activity. These lessons will give you more techniques to use when dramatizing a story.

Personal Notes & Adaptations

Continuing the Story

Overview: Students expand a story beyond its boundaries and create their own additions

Objectives: To stimulate creative and independent thinking
To stimulate logical thinking and problem-solving skills

Grade level: K to 6

Materials: A story

Group size: Small group or entire class

Classroom setup: A circle or a clear space in the front of the room

Procedure & Dialogue

1. Select a story the students have read or have heard, and preset the class.

   '*I'm glad you liked the story of Cinderella. Now let's use our imaginations and take the story a little further.*'

2. Ask them to imagine what might happen to those characters next, after the story ends. Here the story is "Cinderella."

   '*Let's close our eyes and imagine it is five years after Cinderella and the prince were married. What is their life like now? Do they have any children? What does their palace look like? Where is the stepmother? Where are the stepsisters? Where are they living?*'

3. Use visualization or brainstorming techniques to gather a variety of ideas.

   '*Now see a scene in which Cinderella, her stepsisters, and her stepmother are alone. How do they treat each other? What do they say to each other when the Prince is not around? Now let's open our eyes and share what we saw and heard in our imaginations.*'

4. Select several ideas to act out.

   '*Oh . . . I liked a lot of your ideas. Let's act out a few. Let's start with Mark's idea. It's Christmas time and the Prince has gone out shopping with their two children. Cinderella is baking Christmas cookies. She calls her stepmother and stepsisters to come over and help her. Things start out fine, but before long the sisters become more and more jealous of Cinderella and start throwing the cookie dough at her.*'

The stepmother stops the fight, and Cinderella orders everyone to leave. Just then the Prince comes home. Cinderella is covered with cookie dough.'

5. Clear a space, and have the students stand in a circle (see "Role Play, Lessons One, Two, and Three," "Acting Out a Story," "Point of View Switch," and "Object Transformation/ Playbuilding, Lessons Two and Three" for more dramatizing techniques).

   'Let's push back the desks and tables and make a big circle.'

6. Ask questions that motivate the students to retell the story.

   'What scene is first? The Prince leaving with the children.'

7. Assign roles, and begin acting out the story. Feel free to add simple props or a costume piece. Continue to ask questions that allow the students to retell and embellish the story.

   'Okay, who would like to be the Prince? Marcus, please be our Prince. What is the Prince's name? We can't use the name of anyone we know. Fine, Prince Paul it is. Now I need his two children and Cinderella. What are the children's names?'

8. Set up the action and the acting areas.

   'Where does this scene take place? In the kitchen, okay. Cinderella, here is a bowl and a kitchen table for you. We'll pretend this is the kitchen. Here is a cape for the Prince and hats for the children.

   What's going to happen in this scene? Right, Prince Paul decides to go shopping and Cinderella calls her stepsisters and stepmother to come over.

   Where is the Prince coming from? Okay, we'll pretend the bedroom is over here. What can we use as a telephone? The eraser! Good idea.'

9. You may want to get a title for your play before you begin acting it out.

   'What should we call this play? "As the Cookie Crumbles" —great! Are you ready? Scene One of "As the Cookie Crumbles."'

10. You may need to begin as a narrator. Then stop, and let the students speak on their own.

'(As narrator) *It was two weeks before Christmas. Prince Paul came into the kitchen one morning and said . . .*'

11. Add narration if you feel the students are stuck as to what is coming next.

    '(As narrator) *So off the children and Prince Paul went to shop for some presents. Meanwhile, Cinderella decided to make a phone call . . .*'

12. After each scene (or as needed) you can use a control device (see "Acting Out a Story," steps 5 and 6).

    '*FREEZE! Good job—now who do we need? Right, we need the stepmother and sisters.*'

13. Remind them that boys can be girls and vice versa when we are using our imaginations.

    '*Remember—we're just pretending so a boy could be any of these characters. Would any boy like to be the stepmother?*

    Eric, great. Here's a hat for you. Now let me find the stepsisters . . .'

14. If necessary, provide a line of narration, and then let the students do the scene.

    '(As narrator) *So, while Cinderella waited for her stepfamily to arrive, she started rolling out the cookie dough. Suddenly she heard a knock on the door: . .*

    (As narrator) *At first, everyone made cookies, and everyone was very pleasant to each other. They said . . .*

    (As narrator) *But after a while, the sisters' true feelings for Cinderella began to come out . . .*'

15. If the students get carried away, use the control device (see "Acting Out a Story," steps 5 and 6). Ask a question to refocus the group.

    '*FREEZE! Who stops the fight? Right, okay the stepmother stops them. Let's start throwing the imaginary dough again, but be sure you are quiet enough to hear the stepmother speak so she can break up the fight. Let's see the scene.*'

16. Add narration to close the scene.

    '(As narrator) *Just as the stepfamily was leaving, in came the Prince. He saw Cinderella crying and covered with cookie dough and he said . . .*

    (As narrator) *And the stepsisters said . . .*

(As narrator) *And the stepmother said . . .*

(As narrator) *And Cinderella said . . .*

And that's the story of "As the Cookie Crumbles."'

17. Close the activity. You may want to do the story two or three times. You could keep the same cast or change roles. After several times, a student could probably take on the narration as well.

   '*Great job! Give yourselves a hand. Let's do this story one more time, but let's have other students take on the roles.*'

18. Feel free to act out several other ideas as well.

   '*Now let's act out Karen's idea. Karen, tell us again what you saw in your imagination.*'

Activity Extensions

Have the students write or draw their new stories. They can create their own books.

Play old radio dramas for the students and discuss their characteristics. Have the students create their own radio dramas with their ideas.

Videotape any of their plays.

Activity Variations

1. This activity can be modified to use the main character of a story in another adventure.

2. If the environment is a strong factor in a story, have the class create another story in that environment.

3. Use the theme or feelings in the story as a springboard for another story involving the same theme or emotions.

Comments

This is a good prewriting and composing activity.

Personal Notes & Adaptations

Point of View Switch

Overview: Students become various characters in a story and retell the story from their viewpoint

Objectives: To stimulate creative and critical thinking

Grade level: 2 to 6

Materials: A story

Group size: Small group or entire class

Classroom setup: A circle or a clear space in the front of the room

Procedure & Dialogue

1. Select a story the students have read or have heard. Here the story is "Cinderella." (I'm using "Cinderella" as an example again because I assume it is a story with which most readers are familiar, and it works well for both primary- and intermediate-level students.)

2. Preset the class.

   ‘*Today we are going to act out the story of Cinderella, but not the way we read it in our book.*’

3. Ask the students to consider from which character's point of view is the story told.

   ‘*If we were to imagine that a character in Cinderella wrote the story, who would you say wrote it? Right. Probably Cinderella or the Fairy Godmother. If the stepmother wrote the story, would it be the same story? Probably not. So let's imagine some of the other characters in the story, and let's hear them tell their story of Cinderella. We know Cinderella's version of the story, so now let's hear from the stepmother, the stepsisters, the mice, and the pumpkin.*’

4. Assign several students a character from the story to portray. Give them a name tag for the character. Feel free to include even the most minor characters. Have the students acting out a role sit in the front of the room. Eliminate the main character in the story, and let the other characters speak. Ask questions that help the students recall the story.

   ‘*Who would like to be the pumpkin? What did the pumpkin turn into? Right, the carriage. Good. Come up front and sit right here. Here's a name tag and a magic marker. Just hold it for now. What did the mice become in the story? Right, the horses. Who would like to be the mice?'*

5. Assign the remaining students a role as well. For instance, the rest of the class could be news reporters who have come to interview these characters in order to write an article for their newspapers. Give each news reporter a name tag to create a fictional name. You could also give each reporter a 3×5 card and ask them to write on the card one question they'd like to ask each of the characters.

   Another possibility is to create a TV talk-show format. The bulk of the class could be the studio audience, camera people, viewers that call in, commercials, or the microphone. The name tags and 3× 5 cards discussed above could be used for this structure as well. Often the questions are more interesting if the students write them in pairs. Please note:

   a. Do not have the students put on their name tags until everyone is ready to act. This sets up a clear beginning to the fiction (see "Role Play, Lesson Two").

   b. When you first try this activity, you may want to become the talk-show host. It helps keep the activity flowing and on task. Eventually, however, a student may be able to take on this role.

   'Now, those of us that are not up front, I want you to imagine that this is a TV talk show. You are the studio and call-in audience. You get to ask questions of these characters.

   Everyone now has a name tag. Create an imaginary name for yourself and write it on the name tag. If you are an animal, put what kind of animal you are under your name. Those of you playing adults, you may want to write under your name your occupation. Write in big letters, but do not put on the tags yet.

   Audience members, here is an index card. With the person sitting next to you, I want you to write at least one question you want to ask each of the characters up here.

   While you're doing that I need two groups of students to plan a few commercials for our TV show. Who would like to do that? Remember, the commercials have to be for a product you create in your imagination—nothing real.'

6. Give students a few minutes to prepare.

   'Take a few minutes to think through your characters. What are you going to say? You can also get a costume piece or prop out of our box.'

7. Bring the class together, review expectations, and finish details.

'Okay, everyone take their places. Does my studio and call-in audience have their questions ready? Good. Are the commercials ready? Good. Does everyone have their name tags written? I'll be the talk-show host. What should be my name? Remember—we have to think of our own—not one from television. Okay . . . This is the Oprah Losefree Show, and I'll be the host, Oprah Losefree. Sounds good. I'll make my name tag now.'

8. Set up a clear beginning and end to the action. Use visualization to help the students transform into other characters.

'Now close your eyes. When I count to three, those of you in front will imagine that you are the characters in the story. The rest of the class will imagine they are audience members. We may need to sit, act, and talk differently than we normally do. See yourselves as your characters. Our play will be over when I say, "That's all the time we have for today, we'll see you tomorrow." At the count of three, we'll open our eyes, put on our name tags and the show will begin. One . . . two . . . three.'

9. Set the tone by immediately establishing your character.

'(As character) Welcome everyone. Welcome to the Oprah Losefree Show. I'm Oprah Losefree, and today have we got a show for you! Today, the characters from Cinderella are here to tell us what really happened one week ago, the night the clock struck 12.'

10. Interview the characters. You may want to use the imaginary microphone (see "Guidelines for Success").

'(As character) Mike and Margo Mouse, tell us what happened to you that night.

Audience members – who has a question here for Mike or Margo?

Do we have a call-in listener ready with a question?'

11. If the questions asked haven't succeeded in clarifying a character's viewpoint, ask a summary question so that the purpose of the lesson is intact.

'(As character) Mike and Margo, imagine Cinderella is watching the show right now. What would you like to say to her about that night?'

The Creative Classroom

12. Continue with all the characters. After two or three, try to have some break in the action.

'(As character) *And now ladies and gentlemen, we'll be right back after this commercial.*'

13. At times something spontaneous will be said by one character that provokes a response by another character. Use this information.

'(As character) *Stepdaughters, tell us, how do you feel about the fact that your mother just said you would have to start doing all the housework now that Cinderella is gone?*'

14. Bring the play to a clear ending.

'(As character) *That's all the time we have for today, we'll see you all tomorrow.*

(As self) *Close your eyes and at the count of three we will not be characters anymore. We will be ourselves back in our classroom. One . . . two . . . three. Give yourselves a hand.*'

15. A discussion can follow about point of view and what the students discovered through the activity.

Activity Variations

1. A trial is another way to get students to understand that people have varying points of view on an event.

2. You can select only one or two characters and have the students rewrite and/or reenact the story from that character's perspective.

Comments

It may be helpful to read "Role Play, Lessons One, Two, and Three," "Acting Out a Story," "Continuing a Story" and "Objective Transformation/Playbuilding, Lessons Two and Three" before doing this activity. These activities will give you more dramatization ideas.

Personal Notes & Adaptations

8

Strategies for Developing Creative Thinking
Playbuilding (Storybuilding)

Playbuilding is a series of oral composing (storybuilding) activities in which students create their own stories and act them out. I invented this term for the lessons that follow when I developed them as director of the Young People's Theatre at Center Stage, a regional theatre in Baltimore, Maryland.

The strategies that follow assist students in creating and reenacting their own storylines. These techniques require students to use high-level thinking skills as they put it all together. The student must develop a plot, a conflict, motivation, and a resolution. It is an exciting and challenging process to facilitate.

Object Transformation, Lesson 1

Overview: An activity in which students transform real objects into imaginary objects ("Object Transformation, Lesson Two" is a sequel to this lesson.)

Objective: To increase creativity, abstract thinking, vocabulary, and peer cooperation

Grade level: PreK to 6

Materials: An ordinary, but interestingly shaped, object, *e.g.*, scarf (PreK to 2), yardstick (PreK to 2), twisted tree branch (PreK to 6), thick blanket (PreK to 6), a seashell (K to 6)

Group size: Small group or entire class

Classroom setup: Clear space in the front of the room or in a circle

Procedure & Dialogue

1. Select one of the objects listed above from which to work. A scarf is the object used here for grades PreK to two.

2. Show the class the scarf. Begin with reality. Have the children identify the object as a scarf. Talk to the children about the scarf, its uses, properties, color, shape, size, and weight.

   '*What is this really? That's right, it's a scarf. What do you do with a scarf? You can wear it on your head like this. Yes. What color is this scarf? Is it a very big scarf, or just a little scarf? Is it heavy or light? Is it in the shape of a circle, a square, or a triangle?*'

3. Move to fantasy. Tell the children that they can change the scarf into many different things by using their imagination. Show them two or three different possibilities. Try to use the object in a variety of ways, *i.e.*, on the floor as a blanket or beach towel; flat out as a pillow; folded up as a banana, sandwich, or toothbrush; in the air as a flag or a kite. Then ask the children if they would like to turn the scarf into something different.

   '*If I use my imagination, I can turn this scarf into many other things. Would you like to see me do it? What am I pretending it is now? Right, a pillow. And now? Yes, a flag. How about now? Yes, exactly, a banana.*'

4. Have the students come up one by one to transform the object. The other class members guess what transformation has taken place. Give the students three chances to guess, and if they cannot, have the student tell the class what he or she has created. If a student wants to do the activity but doesn't have an idea, give him or her several ideas from which to choose.

    '*Now who would like to come up and turn this object into something different—not a pillow or a flag or a banana, but something completely different?*'

5. Applaud each student.

6. Close the lesson by bringing them back to reality.

    '*You did a great job using your imagination today. Now let's get a little magic dust from behind our ears, and at the count of three we'll throw it and we'll just have a plain old scarf once again. One . . . two . . . three.*'

Comments

Object transformation is a difficult activity for grades PreK to K, but they can do it. Try this activity several times with them. It is a creative process that involves abstract thinking, so it will take some time to develop. The first few times the children may not be able to transform the object themselves, but they can tell you what they would like it to become. On their instructions, you can transform the object for them. Be sure to stress the idea of making something different out of the scarf. Otherwise the children will tend to follow your ideas or the ideas of other classmates.

Activity Extensions

Use "Object Transformation" as a prewriting activity in which the students generate ideas for an oral or written composition (see "Object Transformation, Lessons Two and Three").

Personal Notes & Adaptations

Object Transformation, Lesson 2

Overview: In this activity, students transform real objects into imaginary objects and use these ideas to compose a story line

Objective: To increase creative and abstract thinking
To motivate oral and/or written composition
To promote problem-solving skills

Grade level: PreK to 2

Materials: See "Object Transformation, Lesson One"

Group size: Small group or entire class

Classroom setup: Circle with students in chairs or on the floor

Procedure & Dialogue

1. Follow steps 1 through 5 in "Object Transformation, Lesson One."

2. Transform the object into something magical that can talk. For instance, a yardstick could become a talking magic wand named Wanda or the seashell could become a talking seashell named Sheldon. Here a scarf becomes a talking snake named Natasha.

   '*You did a great job turning the scarf into all sorts of things. But now I'm going to turn this scarf into something magical. Of course it's only magical if we use our imaginations. Right now I'd like to introduce you to a friend of mine, my pet snake, Natasha.*'

3. Make the magical object approachable and kind so that the students will feel safe participating in the activity.

   '*Now, I know some of you may be afraid of snakes, but Natasha is different from other snakes. She doesn't bite or eat other animals; in fact she only eats fruits and vegetables, and her favorite drink is chocolate milk. And you know what? She's very special because she talks . . . of course she only talks if we use our imagination.*'

4. Let each student who wants to "talk" to the object. Do not speak for the object. Let the voice of the object be heard only in the child's imagination. In other words, there is no real voice. Explain that the object only says positive things. (The children will hear amazing things. If possible, let each student listen to the object. If anyone says that the object said something negative, for instance, "*I hate you!*", ask

them to listen again, because the object always says the sweetest things.)

'I think Natasha would like to talk to you. If you want to hear Natasha, just give her a gentle scratch here on the top of the head. Then I'll hold her up to your ear and she will speak to you. She always says the nicest things. She might say, "You're cute" or "I like you." I don't know what she'll say. Emma, give Natasha a little scratch. Now what did she say?'

5. After the students have listened, hold the object to your ear and hear the object cry.

'Natasha, didn't they do a good job? Aren't they a lovely group of children? What's wrong, Natasha? Why are you crying? What happened?'

6. Pretend that the object has indicated to you that there is some sort of problem. The object needs the students to identify the problem and solve it.

'A friend of yours is in trouble and needs our help? What friend is in trouble? Oh, you don't want to tell me—you want to tell one of the students. Who will listen to Natasha and tell us what animal friend of hers needs our help?'

7. These questions may help you in developing your story line. Try if you can to use each idea the students offer in creating the story line. Embellish on their ideas.

Please note: If the students say "Her friend is dead—somebody killed her." I simply reframe the idea by saying: "If her friend is dead, we can't really help her. Could she be hurt?"

If the students want to use violence to solve the problem, I simply indicate that we can't do that. We don't want anyone to get hurt in this story. We have to find another way.

'Is Natasha's friend an animal or a person? Who will listen? Duane, what did she say? It's an animal.

What kind of animal? Valerie, listen.
Oh, it's a snake. It must be her cousin, Sneaky, the snake.

What happened to Sneaky? Lakiesha, what did she say?
Oh . . . she has her tail caught in a door.

How did that happen? Patrice, listen to Natasha.

She was playing hide-and-seek, and she was running really fast, and her tail got caught. Who was she playing with? Anthony, listen.

A pig? Sneaky was playing hide-and-seek with her friend Pinky, the pig.

The Creative Classroom

Where's Pinky now? Why doesn't she help Sneaky? Anna, listen to Natasha.

Oh . . . Pinky is hiding. She doesn't know Sneaky is stuck. She's waiting for Sneaky to find her.

What should we do to help? Nattie, what should we do?

We have to open the door.

What else should we do? Daniel?

Get Sneaky a doctor!

What else should we do? Rebecca?

Find Pinky because she's scared too. She hid in a closet, and she can't get the door open.

Oh! We have a lot to do.

Where do we need to go to help these animals? Ben?

To Sneaky's house?

What color is the house, Ben?

Green. Well, we better get going.'

8. If the object (Natasha) has a part in the story line, then it is important to bring it along on the adventure they are about to act out. However, if possible, I like to leave the item (Natasha) in the classroom so that we can come back and retell the story to the object when we return.

   '*Let's leave Natasha here. We'll tell her all about our adventure when we get back. Does anyone have an imaginary cage we can put her in? Good, Dante, bring it up.*

   What does she like to eat and drink—who remembers? Does anyone have any fruit? Vegetables? Chocolate milk? Great, put them in her cage. Lock the cage Dante—we don't want Natasha wiggling down the hall.'

9. You may want to set up a control device before acting out the story. If so, see steps 5 and 6 in "Acting Out a Story."

10. Use a word, phrase, or sound effect to take the students in and out of the world of fantasy.

    '*This is a musical instrument called a tambourine. When I shake it, if we use our imaginations, we will be at Ben's green house.'*

11. Act out the story. You can assign roles before you begin, do it while the students have their eyes closed, or assign roles as the story unfolds. Often I use a combination of all three

methods. You may want to keep the students in a circle throughout the play so that everyone is able to see. Set up playing areas in the circle. As you facilitate the action, act out the story right along with your students. You may want to take on the role of an authority figure or narrator in the story in order to make your job as director and actor easier.

'Let's stand up and spread out in a nice big circle. Now close your eyes, close your eyes. When I count to three, we'll open our eyes, and we'll see the green house Sneaky lives in, and we'll hear Sneaky crying.

Don't open your eyes yet. I'm looking for two children who are wearing green. (Tap the students and whisper.) Will both of you come over here and make our house?

Now if you would like to be Sneaky in our story, let me know that by keeping your eyes closed, and just raising your hand. Let me see . . . (Tap the students and whisper.) Would you be Sneaky, and would you be the door?

Great, at the count of three, we'll open our eyes and hear Sneaky crying. (Shake tambourine.) One . . . two . . . three.'

12. If one of the children doesn't speak or pick up on a cue, involve the whole group.

   'Let's all be Sneaky crying. Let me hear her.'

13. Use the imaginary microphone and/or magic powder (see "Guidelines for Success") to interview characters. This promotes language. If the character gets stuck and doesn't know what to say, ask the rest of the group "Who remembers what happens next in our story?" Then see if the student will repeat the information.

   Please note: If a character says things that are inappropriate for this story line, I simply take the imaginary microphone away and say, "That is another story, not the one we wrote together today. Do you remember what happens in this story?" This usually gets the student back on track.

   'Oh! There's Sneaky with her tail caught in the door. Andrea, please go and open the door and set Sneaky free. (To group) I'll get out my imaginary microphone here and magic powder. This powder helps animals speak our language so that we can understand them when they talk. I'll sprinkle some on Sneaky. (Place imaginary microphone by Sneaky's mouth) Sneaky, what happened to you? How did that happen? . . .'

14. Try to avoid gender and other stereotypes when casting roles.

'I think Sneaky needs a doctor. Doctor Lakiesha, will you take a look a Sneaky's tail? What's wrong with her? What can you do?'

15. Ask questions that remind the class of the sequence of the story.

'Well, I think Sneaky's okay, but who do we need to take care of now?

Right, Pinky. Where is she?

In the closet. Could the four of you make the closet? Would you be the closet door, and Alicia will you be Pinky, the pig? We need to hear you crying, too. Why is she crying?

Right, because she can't get the door open. Let's see all of that, Alicia. Max, will you come and open the door for Pinky?

(To group) Let me just sprinkle some magic dust here and get out my microphone.

Pinky, what happened? Are you all right?

Here's Sneaky—she was crying too. Who will tell Pinky what happened to Sneaky?

Let's tell Pinky and Sneaky who sent us here to help them— who remembers her name?

Right, Natasha.'

16. Close the story with questions that promote courtesy and language.

'Pinky and Sneaky, what do you want to say to Natasha and all of us for helping you? Do you have any other messages for Natasha?
What do we want to say to Pinky and Sneaky?

Well, let's say good-bye—Good-bye . . .

Close your eyes, close your eyes, because at the count of three, we'll be back in the classroom, and we'll tell Natasha the whole story. One . . . two . . . three.'

17. Retell the story, if possible in sequence.

'Well, we're back! Dante, bring over the key to your cage, and I'll get Natasha. Oh, she ate the fruit and vegetables and drank all the milk. Here, Dante, you can take your cage now.

Who will tell Natasha where we went? Who did we find? What did we do? Then what did we do?'

18. Close the activity.

> '*Well, I think Natasha wants to go home now. Let's say good-bye to Natasha. Now close your eyes because at the count of three, Natasha will be gone and we'll just have a plain old scarf. One . . . two . . . three.* (Shake tambourine.) *Great job. Give yourselves a hand.*'

Activity Extensions

Students can then draw or write this story. They can create their own books.

Students can create another story line using the same characters.

Comments

The magical item can return over and over to create other story lines. You can even focus the story to fit a unit or theme presently being studied. For instance, a kindergarten class was studying African animals, and so I turned Natasha into an African snake who missed her friends at home. We flew to Africa and met all her friends. The children loved becoming all of the different African animals. They all had lovely things to say to Natasha on her visit home.

Sheldon, the talking seashell, is great for underwater adventures.

Wanda, the magic wand (a yard stick), can be used in endless ways. She can even make wishes come true.

If you need a magic chant in the play, have the students create their own. Don't let them use any chants from books, TV, or movies. You'd be surprised what they come up with.

You may find it helpful to read "Role Play, Lessons One, Two and Three"; "Acting Out a Story"; "Continuing a Story"; "Point of View Switch"; and "Object Transformation, Lessons One and Three" before doing this lesson. These lessons will provide more ideas for dramatization.

Please note: I want these playbuilding lessons to have a positive tone and to be uplifting experiences for students. To achieve this goal, I try to include characters who need the students' help in some way, and I eliminate violence as a problem-solving solution. I find that in doing this, I can tap into students' ability to feel compassion, and I can elevate the level of creative thinking.

Personal Notes & Adaptations

Object Transformation, Lesson 3

Overview: In this activity, students transform real objects into imaginary objects and use these ideas to compose a story line

Objective: To increase creative and abstract thinking
To motivate oral and/or written composition
To promote problem-solving skills

Grade level: 1 to 6

Materials: See "Object Transformation, Lesson One"

Group size: Small group or entire class

Classroom setup: Circle with students in chairs or on the floor

Procedure & Dialogue

1. Follow steps 1 through 5 in "Object Transformation, Lesson One." However, for this lesson, instead of a scarf I am using a twisted branch of a tree.

2. As each student looks at the object and transforms it into something different, write their ideas on chart paper or on the board.

   '*Ernesto, what does the tree branch look like to you? Deer antlers. Good, let me add that to our list. Who sees something different?*'

3. After the class has generated a list of 15 to 20 items, circle three to six of the most interesting items to create a story. These items may relate in some way or they may not. You may want to circle items that would give your story a setting and a cast of characters. You may want to ask the class to choose the items.

   '*We have a lot of ideas here, and we're going to use some of these ideas to create our play. We can't use all of these ideas or our story will be too confusing, so let's choose five ideas; which ones should we include? All right, I've circled deer antlers, the number seven, a twisty road, a fire, and lightning.*'

4. Create a story using these items. Feel free to start the story yourself or let the students start the story. If you start the story, develop the story up to a point of conflict, and then let the students solve the problem.

Try to create story lines that lend themselves to positive results. Try to create plots in which someone or something is in need of help or plots in which the feeling of compassion is evoked.

'I'm going to start the play, and I'll need you to help finish the story. It was a beautiful summer night, and so the camp director at Camp Twisty Road decided to take all of her best campers on an overnight up the twisty road into the mountains. She decided to take only those campers who knew a lot about nature and really loved animals and the wilderness.

When they got to the top of the mountain, the camp director asked everyone to gather some kindling to make a fire. The campers built the campfire and sat around singing songs, when suddenly one of the branches in the campfire turned into a golden set of deer antlers and, to everyone's shock, the antlers began to talk. They said, "Thank you for coming. I have waited a long time. I need your help. Follow me."'

5. Use questions to embellish and finish the story. You may need to call on several students in order to get a solid idea. Try to incorporate as many ideas as you can. Remind the students to use any of the remaining circled items from the list on the board.

   Please note: If the students want to use violence to solve the problem, I simply say that we can't do that. No one can get hurt in this story. We'll have to find another way. I also do not let students use characters or ideas from TV or movies.

   'What kind of help did the antlers need?

   The golden deer who owned these antlers was in trouble. What kind of trouble?

   Ah, lightning struck a tree. The tree fell on the deer, breaking off his antlers and trapping the deer.

   So where are the antlers taking us? To the deer.

   What are we supposed to do? Lift the tree off the deer.

   How will we put the antlers back on? How can we make them stay?

   With a magic chant the deer will teach us.
   Let's write that chant now, and it can't be anything you have heard or read before. Let's see if we can get the number 7 in our chant . . .'

6. Conclude the story.

'What magical powers does this deer have? Oh, he is King of the Forest and he protects the animals from harm. If the campers save him, what gift could he leave with the campers? Let's come up with a gift that isn't money, and can't be used to buy anything. What gift could he give?'

7. You may want to set up a control device before acting out the story. If so, see steps 5 and 6 in "Acting Out a Story."

8. Act out the story (see step 10 in "Object Transformation, Lesson Two" before proceeding). Assign parts and set up the playing areas.

'You've written a great story. Let's stand and act it out. I'll be the camp director. What should be my name? We can't use the name of anyone we know.

Okay, my name will be Mrs. Woods. Who would like to be the golden talking antlers? Who would like to be the golden deer? Who will be the tree? When it's time, we'll put the tree over here.'

9. Involve all the students in the action.

'We'll all be the campers.'

10. Use a word, phrase, or sound effect to begin and end the action. This helps the students move from reality to fantasy and back to reality.

'Now when I play these three notes on my xylophone, we'll leave our classroom and go to Camp Twisty Road. So close your eyes, close your eyes, because when you hear those three notes, we'll be at Camp Twisty Road, and I'll be the camp director, Mrs. Woods. One . . . two . . . three.'

11. Immediately take on the character, and set the tone for the play. If possible, change your voice and posture.

Please note: If any student tries to change the story or is uncooperative, simply stop the action (use control devices, steps 5 and 6 in "Acting Out a Story") and remind the student what he or she is doing isn't a part of this story. Remind them they are acting out the story they just wrote today.

'(As Mrs. Woods) Oh, what a beautiful night. I'll tell you what . . . I called all of you together—my wisest campers— because I know how much you love nature, and, well, I thought you'd like to climb up the mountain for an overnight. Doesn't that sound great? So let's go.'

12. Ask questions to embellish the story.

   'What should we take with us? What else do we need?'

13. Give hints and ask leading questions so that the students provide most of the story line. Keep the students in a circle so that everyone can see and no one is trampled upon.

   'Well, let's put on all our gear and start climbing . . .

   Ohh . . . it's kind of cold up here on the mountain top. What should we do? Go and gather some wood for a fire, and put it all right here. Let's sit in a big circle around the fire.

   What should we do now? Great idea—let's sing some songs. What should we sing?'

14. When the story is completed use the same word, phrase, or sound effect (see step 10) to end the story.

   'Close your eyes, close your eyes, because when I play these notes on my xylophone, our play will be over, and we'll be back in our room, and we'll give ourselves a hand for acting. One . . . two . . . three.'

Activity Extensions

1. Discuss with the students any parts of the story that are not clearly resolved. Use these ideas as a springboard for another play or for a writing assignment.

   'What things are still unclear about this story? What do you think happens to the deer next? What did the campers do with the deer's gift? Who needs the deer's magical powers?'

2. Have the students create their own books and/or movie or video.

Activity Variations

1. After the class transforms the object(s), break the class into groups. Have each group select five or six items, create their own story, rehearse it, and present it to the class.

2. The students can also write their plays in script form.

Comments

It may be helpful to read "Role Play, Lessons One, Two, and Three" in Chapter 6; "Acting Out a Story"; "Continuing a Story"; "Point of View Switch"; and "Object Transformation, Lesson Two" before doing this lesson. They will give you more dramatizing techniques.

This activity is endless in its possibilities and students love it.

Personal Notes & Adaptations

Conclusion

I hope that in reading this book you have found many activities that are useful for you to use in your classroom. I also hope that these techniques sparked your creativity and prompted you to develop your own creative drama games.

Here is a lesson plan outline that may help you integrate these techniques into your daily routine. The more you use these activities, the more comfortable you will feel, and the more creative you will become.

CREATIVE DRAMA LESSON PLAN

Subject Area:

Grade Level:

   I.   Concept to be taught
   II.   Objectives/outcomes
   III.   Creative drama activities
   IV.   Materials
   V.   Motivation
   VI.   Procedure & Dialogue
   VII.   Evaluation
   VIII.   Creative drama extension activities
   IX.   Comments
   X.   Personal notes and adaptations

In addition to all the reasons I stated in the introduction for using creative drama in the classroom, the best reason came directly from one of my low-ability high school students. Several years after he had graduated, he turned up as a waiter in a restaurant where my husband and I just happened to be eating.

My husband asked Bob how he would describe my teaching style. To my surprise, Bob said, "Well, we always had a good time, but we always learned something."

For me, that's the best answer he could have given! I hope that through this book you and your students have a good time and learn something as well.

Bibliography

Bright, Deborah, M.D. 1979. *Creative Relaxation*. New York: Harcourt Brace Jovanovich, Inc.

Burger, Isabelle. 1950. *Creative Play Acting*. New York: A.S. Barnes and Company.

Cambique, Susan. 1981. *Learning through Dance/Movement*. Los Angeles: Performing Tree, Inc. Published by Los Angeles Unified School District.

Champlin, Connie. 1980. *Puppetry and Creative Drama in Storytelling*. Austin, Texas: Nancy Renfro Studios.

Cook, Wayne. 1993. *Center Stage, K–3*. Palo Alto, California: Dale Seymour Publications.

Cottrell, June. 1984. *Teaching with Creative Dramatics*. Lincolnwood, Illinois: National Textbook Company.

Cranston, Jerneral W. 1991. *Transformations through Drama*. Lanham, Maryland: University Press of America, Inc.

Cullum, Albert. 1967. *Push Back the Desks*. New York: Citation Press.

Fox, Mem. 1987. *Teaching Drama to Young Children*. Portsmouth, NH: Heinemann.

Glub, Jeff. 1986. *Activities to Promote Critical Thinking*. Urbana, Illinois: National Council of Teachers of English.

Have You Roared Today? 1979. Rockville, Maryland: Montgomery County Public Schools, Title I, ESEA.

Heinig, Ruth Beall. 1987. *Creative Drama Resource Book for Grades 4 through 6*. Englewood Cliffs, New Jersey: Prentice-Hall.

————. 1987. *Creative Drama Resource Book for Kindergarten through Grade 3*. Englewood Cliffs, New Jersey: Prentice-Hall.

———. 1992. *Improvisation with Favorite Tales: Integrating Drama into the Reading/Writing Classroom*. Portsmouth, New Hampshire: Heinemann.

Kase-Polisini, Judith. 1989. *The Creative Drama Book: Three Approaches*. New Orleans: Anchorage Press.

Kraus, Joanna H. 1971. *Sound and Motion Stories*. Rowayton, Connecticut: New Plays.

McCaslin, Nellie. 1987. *Creative Drama in the Intermediate Grades*. White Plains, New York: New York University, Longman, Inc.

McCaslin, Nellie. 1987. *Creative Drama in the Primary Grades*. White Plains, New York: New York University, Longman, Inc.

Nagy, William E. 1988. *Teaching Vocabulary to Improve Reading Comprehension*. Urbana, Illinois: National Council of Teachers of English.

O'Neill, Cecily, and Alan Lambert. 1982. *Drama Structures*. Portsmouth, New Hampshire: Heinemann.

Postman, Neil. 1982. *The Disappearance of Childhood*. New York: Dell Publishing.

Schwartz, Dorothy, and Dorothy Aldrich, eds. 1986. *Give Them Roots and Wings,* 2nd ed. New Orleans: Anchorage Press.

Siks, Geraldine Brain. 1960. *Creative Dramatics: An Art for Children*. New York: Harper and Row.

Spolin, Viola. 1963, 1983. *Improvisation for the Theatre*. Evanston, Illinois: Northwestern University Press.

———. 1989. *Theatre Game File*. Evanston, Illinois: Northwestern University Press.

———. 1986. *Theatre Games for the Classroom*. Evanston, Illinois: Northwestern University Press.

Stewig, John Warren. 1983. *Informal Drama in the Elementary Language Arts Program*. New York: Teachers College Press.

Swartz, Larry. 1988. *DramaThemes, A Practical Guide for Teaching Drama*. Portsmouth, New Hampshire: Heinemann.

Ward, Winifred. 1957. *Playmaking with Children*. New York: Appleton Century Crofts.

Watson, Dorothy J. 1987. *Ideas and Insights, Language Arts in the Elementary School*. Urbana, Illinois: National Council of Teachers of English.

Way, Brian. 1972. *Development through Drama*. New York: Humanities Press.